BALLET
How It All Began

Vivian Werner

BALLET

How It All Began

ILLUSTRATED WITH
OLD PRINTS & PHOTOGRAPHS

1982 ATHENEUM New York

PICTURE CREDITS

*We are grateful to the following sources for permission to reproduce
the pictures in this book:*

Bibliothèque Nationale; pages 19, 56, 65, 83

*George Chaffee collection, Harvard Theatre Collection
frontispiece and pages 62, 70, 76*

*French Cultural Services; pages 6, 14–15, 18, 22,
27, 33, 78, 80*

The Library of Congress; page 85

*The New York Public Library at Lincoln Center,
Dance Collection; pages 47, 71, 87, 92, 94, 103, 106, 107*

*The New York Public Library Picture Collection;
pages 9, 41, 53, 68, 72, 98, 113, 115*

W. W. Norton and Company, Inc.; pages 20–21, 100

LIBRARY OF CONGRESS CATALOGING IN PUBLICATION DATA

*Werner, Vivian L.
Ballet, how it all began.*

SUMMARY: *Traces the development of ballet from
its roots in fifteenth-century France and Italy
to the present day.
1. Ballet—History—Juvenile literature. [1. Ballet
History] I. Title.
GV 1787.5.W 47   792.8'09   81-8093
ISBN 0-689-30908-2   AACR2*

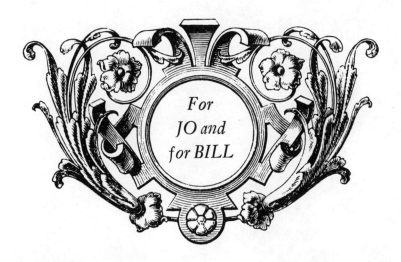

For
JO and
for BILL

Like The Comic Ballet of Queen Louise, *this lavish early 17th-century ballet was based on the characters of classic myths.*

ACKNOWLEDGEMENTS

I have had special help from very special people in writing & researching this book, and I want to give them my special thanks:

To Merrill Lindsay, for sharing his expertise on ancient arms with me. To Mark Platt, my first ballet teacher. To Carl Balestracci, Sr., for explaining the intricacies of fencing. To Robert Vickery, of the Connecticut Ballet, for guidance in tracing the history of dance. To Debi Testa, both for defining technical terms and demonstrating techniques. And to Susie Engelman, for patiently reading my manuscript and for continually encouraging me.

I am, as well, deeply grateful to those many great dancers and remarkable teachers who permitted me to join their classes and from whom I learned—not to dance—but what dance was: Martha Graham, Martha Hill, the late Mary Anne Wells, Bonnie Byrd, the late Syvilla Fort, Erick Hawkins and the late José Limón, as well as the late composer, Louis Horst.

BALLET
How It All Began

T HIS IS THE STORY *of a battle and of how that battle was lost. It is the story of ballet, too. And it tells why—because that battle was lost—dance is what it is today.*
The story began over 500 years ago—in the year 1415—near a castle in France called Agincourt.

THE ENGLISH SOLDIERS were weary. Day after day they had marched across the French countryside. Now only a few could even count the number of days that had passed. Fewer still could count the miles. But all knew that it had been three months since they had set sail from their own shores.

They were eight thousand strong then. And their King, Henry V, was at their head. Their goal was to win back for him the lands he claimed as his own in France.

All had been ready to die for their sovereign. And many already had. Some had fallen in battle. Others had died of disease. Now fewer than three thousand were left. None—not even the king—was eager to fight.

But word came that the French armies were gathering nearby. If King Henry did not make some show of force, he would seem to be a coward.

A show of force did not mean a battle, though. King Henry could save his honor if he only provoked the French. He could do that by marching his army through the region they both claimed. If he outdistanced the French, as he planned to, he could avoid war and still protect his good name. And once he reached the port city of Calais, which was held by the English, he and his men would be safe.

They were almost there when French heralds appeared at Henry's camp. They had a message; it was a challenge to fight. And it proved that the enemy was close on his heels.

With no time to lose, Henry ordered the English army to set out at once. Then he hurried his men along, giving them almost no rest.

But very soon Henry had more bad news. The French armies had caught up with him. They did not attack, though. They simply marched along, keeping pace with the English soldiers.

Henry still hoped to escape—he could almost see Calais—when the worst news of all was brought to him. The French had crossed his path and cut him off. Now they waited just ahead, drawn up ready for battle.

Henry would have ordered his men into battle formation, too. But it was growing dark, so they settled down to wait.

When night fell, the French broke ranks. Like the English, they settled down to wait for dawn. There would have to be a battle then. It could not be postponed forever.

It was a long and dreary night for the English troops. The rain beat down on their heads. It soaked their clothes. The cold wind chilled them to the bone. And many were hungry, too. They had used up their rations days before. Now they had very little to eat beside the few nuts and berries they could gather. Worse, still, they were tormented by fears of the coming battle.

The English soldiers knew it would not be an even match. For every one of them, twenty would fight for France. For every horse the English had, the French had ten. Moreover the French—men and horses alike—wore heavy armor plate, made from forged and hammered steel. They would be well-protected.

Morning came at last. With dawn, the French pages woke their knights and helped them to dress.

They fastened heavy breastplates over their chests. They fastened other plates to their backs. And to both—the breastplates and the backplates—they fastened skirts of steel.

They placed steel yokes on the shoulders of the French knights. They fastened steel collars around their necks. They covered their thighs with steel.

They buckled steel kneepieces around their knees. They fastened steel sleeves around the knights' arms.

They slid their hands into steel gloves. They wrapped steel around their legs and forced their feet into metal shoes with curved and pointed toes. And they set helmets —broad-brimmed and made of steel—on their heads.

While the pages helped the knights dress, grooms attended to the horses. They draped richly-colored saddle cloths over their backs. They strapped on their velvet-covered saddles.

Heavy armor weighed down the French; pointed shoes kept knights from standing.

They put steel masks over the horses' heads. They put steel shields over their chests. And at last, both horses and knights were prepared for battle.

Then the pages and the grooms and the squires lifted the knights into their saddles because their armor was so heavy that they could not mount their horses themselves. Finally, they handed them the reins and gave them the long, spearlike lances they would carry.

The English men-at-arms were also up at the break of day. And like the French nobles, they too dressed for battle.

But few of the English had armor. Those who did had only light chain mail, made of iron, not steel. It lined their long, quilted vests. A few also had chain mail leggings. But the archers, the mainstays of the English army, had no armor of any kind.

Like the men-at-arms, they wore long, quilted vests. Like them they wore helmets. But theirs had no brims. And they fitted close to their heads like some sort of strange bucket.

Instead of the swords carried by the men-at-arms, the archers carried bows and arrows. Each carried an ax or a sledge hammer, too. And each had a long stick with a sharp point at either end.

When the French were ready, they gathered—by the thousands—at one end of the muddy battlefield. When the sun came out, their armor flashed and sparkled. When the breezes blew, their bright-colored banners flapped and snapped.

The French knights were cheerful, certain of victory. They laughed and shouted; they ate and drank. And they pushed and shoved and struggled for positions in the front row. Those who led the attack from such positions would be best placed to capture an English knight and to gain glory for themselves. If it was at the expense of their own comrades, it mattered little. Personal glory was the sole aim of each.

As they waited, their horses, draped in cloth to match the banners and adorned with many-colored plumes, pawed the ground. They were as impatient for the battle to begin as their riders were.

Across the field, a thin line of English knights on horseback, a thin line of English archers and an even thinner line of men-at-arms faced the French. They were hungry and tired and thirsty. Some were sick. All were restless as they waited for the order to attack. It did not come for hours.

At last the call rang out and the archers moved forward. When they were near enough the French to shoot arrows into their enemies' ranks they stopped. Then each drove his two-pointed stick into the ground before him.

The archers drew their bows again and waited for another signal. When it came, their arrows flew through the air. They struck the armor of the French with a clatter.

The French knights charged at once. They stood tall in their saddles and dug their heels into the flanks of their horses. They held their lances in front of them, forming a straight and steady line of pointed steel. They raced across the field, pressed so close together that their knees touched.

The archers shot again. Often, their arrows glanced off the heavy plate. But here and there one passed through the chinks in the armor.

Here and there a knight toppled to the ground; here

1400–1500. Archers wore long, quilted vests and helmets without brims, and so were less burdened than armored knights on horseback.

and there a horse was killed. But the others galloped on, headed for the rows of sharp spikes planted in the ground.

When the horses saw them, it was too late. Some shied and reared back, throwing their riders. Some could not stop. They fell on the spikes and were killed. Others stumbled over those that had fallen. They fell, too.

Those knights who were still in their saddles turned their horses when they saw what had happened. They spurred them to the rear. But they were met at once by their own foot soldiers, marching shoulder-to-shoulder in row after solid row.

The foot soldiers—men-at-arms—in the front line stopped short. Those behind, though, could not see the fallen horses; they marched on. Soldiers further behind pressed against them. They tripped and fell over those already on the ground. Soon the battlefield was piled high with French knights and horses and men-at-arms.

Knights who toppled from their horses could not mount them again by themselves. And now there was no one to lift them to their saddles.

Those who could stand could not walk because of their strange, pointed shoes. And many who fell—both knights and men-at-arms—could not even pull themselves to their feet. The ground was too wet, too slippery; their armor was too heavy. And so they lay there, struggling.

The English archers dropped their bows and arrows then and ran onto the field swinging axes and hammers. Sometimes alone, sometimes in groups of two or three, they attacked their foes.

The French could not move quickly enough to dodge blows or to duck them. They could not defend themselves with their own weapons.

Their lances were so long that they struck their comrades, standing at a distance. They could not hit the English standing close by. They had no room to fight as they were trained to.

Above all, the French could not keep their balance.

And so the battle was over quickly. Many of the French were taken prisoner. Many more were killed. A powerful army of heavily armed noblemen was defeated by a handful of ragged soldiers with nothing but bows and arrows and axes.

The archers were no braver than the knights. They were not even more skillful. But they were nimble and quick. They were sure-footed. And so, there at Agincourt, they won the battle.

THE WAR ENDED AT LAST. The English soldiers sailed for home. And in London, a joyous celebration welcomed them.

The King was honored at a great banquet. After it, a pageant was presented. It was held outdoors so that all—the soldiers and the people of the city, too—could enjoy it.

How they cheered when musicians and actors and dancers appeared! They all wore splendid costumes—more splendid than any had seen before. And they acted out scenes of battle under the cloudless sky. The greatest moment came when a group of players, dressed as soldiers, stormed the walls of a city. The city was only imaginary. When it was captured, though, the crowd clapped and whistled and shouted until everyone was hoarse.

It was far different, though, for the French. Their hearts were heavy as they returned to their homes. Many of their companions were dead; many more were wounded. They grieved for all.

Moreover, only a few who escaped without injury had captured English knights. So only these few won glory on the field of battle. And even they smarted under their defeat because the defeat was at the hands of common soldiers and not at the hands of nobles. Yet the French were far from giving up or from giving in. After all, they were noblemen. And noblemen were sworn to uphold certain traditions.

Those were the traditions of chivalry. They bound nobles to protect the people who served them. The peasants who tilled their fields; the women who worked in their households. The cobblers who made their boots; the tinkers who mended their pots. It was the duty of the noble to protect each of them.

And so the noble must be a sturdy soldier. He must be skilled in battle. He had always gained those skills at jousting matches. It was there—at the tourney, or the tournament—that he had a chance to practice for war.

The tourney entertained the noble, too. When one was held, knights and nobles, along with their squires and pages, were drawn to it from near and far. And because it lasted for several days, all pitched their tents before the castle of their host.

They feasted on the tasty foods he provided. They drank his meads and ales. And when they had their fill, they went off to the lists where the match took place.

Most of them, along with their ladies, climbed into the stands around the lists. But the bravest of the knights mounted their horses and rode onto the field. Holding their lances in their mailed fists, they trotted around the enclosure.

To a knight, gallantry was as important as valor. He proved his gallantry by the courtesy he showed a lady. So he stepped before the one he admired the most and saluted her. The lady answered with a nod or a wave of her hand.

A tourney—only a game—prepared knights for war,

where they were in deadly earnest.

Sometimes she tossed her scarf or her kerchief to the knight, too. If so, he tied it to his lance like a pennant. As it flew in the breeze it spurred him on to victory.

And victory went to the knight who broke the lance of his foe or sent it flying from his hand, or, better still, unseated him. But the knight did not try to capture his opponent. He did not try to kill him. This was only a tourney, and not a real battle.

In other ways, though, the two were very much alike. Just as in battle, each knight on horseback faced another knight on horseback. Between the two lay a wide field. And the knights at a tourney, like those in battle, fretted as they waited for the signal to attack. It was sounded by pages, dressed in hose of silk and doublets of the brightest hue. Banners of the same colors hung from the long, gleaming trumpets they held to their lips. The blast from those trumpets sent the nobles hurtling towards one another.

The visors of their helmets were closed, to protect their faces. Their bodies were protected by armor and by the shields they carried. The lances they held before them, lighter than those used for war, had blunted ends.

There was a clash of metal against metal, and perhaps the sound of splintering wood as the knights crossed weapons in the center of the field. A storm of dust rose and swirled around them. When it settled, the knights' squires ran onto the field. They picked up the fallen lances and handed them back to their lords. Or they replaced broken ones with new. And if a knight had fallen, the squire helped him from the field.

Three times the nobles tilted at one another. If one fell or lost his lance or saw it shattered, the other was the clear-cut winner. If the match seemed even, the judges decided the outcome and awarded the coveted prize.

That was the tournament two centuries before the battle of Agincourt. It was a source of amusement to the entire countryside. It was a training ground, too. It was a place where a knight developed his strength and practiced his skills.

But, as the French discovered to their sorrow at Agincourt, the lance had become too unwieldy for use in battle. Huge swords weighed the nobles down at a time when their very lives depended on their being quick. And those who used their bludgeons were likely to be thrown off balance when a fall might easily mean death.

The heavy weapons became a hindrance. The skills the noble learned through jousting no longer served him. The strength he developed—like that of a bull—counted for little. In future battles the knight would learn to defend himself with light armor and a light rapier rather than the heavy, two-bladed sword he had always carried.

In a duel or a fencing match with the new weapon, victory went to the knight who was graceful and light and elegant. And those were just the qualities the nobles had long developed through the dance.

Nothing pleased the French nobles more than dancing. They liked balls as much as they liked tournaments. It was there that they could display their fine manners. It was there that they could woo some lovely lady. A ball in the great hall of a castle made the evening pass quickly. Sometimes the lord of a neighboring castle paid a visit, bringing his lady and his guests. Troubadours—singers and actors, poets and acrobats—might knock at the gate. In return for food and shelter, they entertained everyone. After the troubadours retired to their corner by the fire, the nobles

1400–1500. Nights in castles passed quickly with games to play, jesters to watch— and dancing to follow.

led their ladies onto the floor of the hall. They held them lightly by the hand as they guided them through the steps of a favorite dance.

It was always slow and stately. The ladies wore such heavy gowns with such long trains that they could not move quickly. Sometimes they only stood in place, swaying slightly or tapping their feet.

The dances of the nobles were borrowed from the dances of the peasants who worked in their fields. The music, the rhythms, even the steps they performed were almost the same. And yet how different they were!

1100–1200. Peasants, sometimes barefoot, danced in the fields; the nobles borrowed their dances and took them into the ballrooms.

1550–1600. When peasants danced, they had no grace . . .

Peasants kicked up their heels and swung their arms. Lords and ladies danced with great dignity. Peasants were often loose-jointed. Nobles controlled each gesture. And peasants were often so exuberant that they tripped over their own feet. Nobles, though, danced with grace and ease. They were vain and proud. They spent hours in the saddle and so they had fine, slender figures they loved to show off. Because the nobles did no work, their hands were soft and white. They loved to show them off, too. And they carried themselves as if they had no fear. They held their backs straight, their heads high. They thrust out their chests. They pulled their shoulders back. Noblemen expected to be seen and to be admired, especially by the ladies.

All were proud, but the proudest was the king. And because he was king, all the others imitated him. They even imitated the way he walked. The king walked with his feet turned out. Like him, the noblemen turned their feet out, too. Like him, they strutted the way peacocks do when they display their marvelous feathers, touching the floor first with their toes, then their heels.

The manners of the nobles were very grand. Their fashionable clothes were richly decorated. When they moved, it was in a majestic way. And they were most ele-

but lords and ladies were dignified.

gant when they danced. They stepped lightly in their castles, keeping their feet close to the floor.

But the floors of the early castles were made of stone and far too rough to skim across swiftly. Then, around the twelfth century, stone floors were replaced with floors of polished wood. The nobles could truly glide over them. And so the style of dance changed. It became lighter and more graceful.

A hundred years later, when the roads around the castles were paved with cobblestones, dance changed again. Until then, the roads had been nothing but packed mud. And the shoes people wore were made of suede so soft that they were almost like socks. Even the soles were made of suede.

The new cobblestones cut through the soft soles when the nobles walked along the roads. And so, to protect their feet, they began to make their shoes of leather. That used for the shoe itself was supple, but the leather used for the soles was much stiffer.

This fine shoe leather came from Spain and was very expensive. Servants kept it bright and gleaming by polishing the shoes of their masters many times a day. Bad weather, though, often ruined the handsome footwear. Rain washed dirt over the roads and turned them into

Clogs protected the nobles' fine shoes from mud and dust.

muddy rivers. Those muddy rivers splattered and stained the shoes. During a dry spell, layers of dust covered the roads. It drifted over the shoes and cracked them.

Just as the nobles found a way to protect their feet— by wearing leather shoes—they found a way to protect the shoes themselves. They protected them by attaching strips of wood, or clogs to the soles.

At first, the clogs could be removed. Later they were attached permanently. They were heavy, though, and clumsy. And so the nobles began to make them smaller.

And smaller.

And smaller still, until finally the clogs were nothing more than heels, like those on shoes today. But such a change took many, many years. It was not until the middle of the fifteenth century that clogs completely disappeared.

With their new heels the nobles—and their ladies— stood taller. That added to their pride; it put a new spring into their steps. So they moved still more easily, more quickly, more gracefully, both when they walked and when they danced.

Yet the ladies were still hampered by their heavy robes. To be as graceful as their partners, they shortened their trains. Then they gave them up completely. They would not give up their jewels, though, no matter how heavy they were. The ladies were as vain as their lords. But now they were clad in gowns of silk instead of the heavy woolen ones they had worn before. And so they, too, moved with a new grace and ease.

For nearly three hundred years—from the twelfth century to the fifteenth century—dance had been changing. At the end of that time it was no longer so slow and stately that people seemed scarcely to move. At the end of it both nobles and their ladies took tiny, running steps. They jumped or sometimes even hopped. This was only possible when they were no longer hampered by heavy clothes, by rough stone floors, or by clumsy shoes.

Once they rid themselves of those clothes and replaced stone floors with floors of polished wood and attached real heels to their shoes, they learned to be quick and nimble and light on their feet. And those were just the skills they needed to handle the thin-bladed, flexible rapier. They were just the skills they needed for fencing.

So, after Agincourt, when the jousting match lost its popularity as entertainment because the joust was no longer useful to train knights for battle, dancing took its place. Every day, each knight and noble practiced his steps under the watchful eye of his dancing master. Each day, too, he practiced dueling under the eye of the fencing master who also lived in the castle.

The knight, the noble, had to become expert in both fencing and in dance. Only then would he be considered a gentleman.

NOT ALL GENTLEMEN lived at courts, as attendants there. So not all gentlemen were courtiers. But all courtiers —those who did live in their sovereigns' castles—were gentlemen. They had the finest possible manners.

Most were of noble birth. Some were lords or counts. Some were barons. Some were even princes. And all were knights as well, since they served their King in time of war.

But courtiers did more than fight for their ruler. They also advised him, both in affairs of state and in personal matters. Some managed his estates; others managed his money. All, though, rode into battle behind his flag if called to do so.

Although they did not put aside their heavy armor completely until the beginning of the seventeenth century, they wore it less and less. At Agincourt, they learned that it was a hindrance. And they discovered that it gave them little defense against firearms, which appeared after gunpowder was introduced into Europe at the beginning of the fourteenth century. So the nobles wore their suits of mail only on special occasions.

The grandest of them dressed in armor to have their

portraits painted. They were clad in it when they rode into the lists for a jousting match. For the most part though, the suits of armor simply stood in the great halls of the great castles, beneath the portraits and the shields that hung on the walls.

Yet courtiers still upheld the ideals of chivalry. They were still true to its traditions. If they were noblemen, they still ruled over all who lived on their lands, and they carried out their duty to protect the weak and the poor.

Those were lawless days and France—like other countries—was a lawless land. So the knights and nobles—and courtiers—laid down their own rules and meted out justice to any who disobeyed. They put murderers to death. They punished those common criminals who committed common crimes—the peasants who stole from other peasants, the poachers who shot the landowner's deer or caught fish from his rivers. Often they put them to death, too.

For all their fine manners, the nobles were brutal. For all their fine manners, they were cruel. They kept order in the land, but they kept it by means of the sword.

They were gentle with the ladies of their own class, though, kind to them and courteous. That, too, was in the tradition of chivalry, and it helped them to forget the horrors of the times.

Evil surrounded the knights and nobles. People died from terrible diseases. Men were killed for a handful of grain. Others were tortured to death. There was suffering everywhere. In such a world, only the noblewomen seemed pure and good. And so the courtiers honored and respected them. They spent their lives trying to prove that they were worthy of their love.

The noble wooed his lady with poetry and music. He

*The traditions of chivalry were made truly royal in this
fifteenth-century wedding procession of a prince and his princess.*

serenaded her from beneath her balcony by moonlight. He sent her verses he wrote for her. He sent them, though, by messenger. It was not considered proper for a courtier to approach his lady himself. It was rare that he was even close enough to his beloved to speak to her.

If the two were together, the lady was not alone. Her mother or her married sister or—if she were still very young—her nurse was near by. So the knight could hold his true love's hand only when they danced. Only then could he whisper sweet words into her ear.

So to win his lady fair, the courtier had to be an expert dancer. He had to seem to move without effort, to be as light as a bird on the wing.

He had to know every step, every movement of each dance, too, and know them perfectly. The knight who stumbled or took a false step might lose his lady to another knight, one more graceful than he. Moreover, to compete with the other knights, he also had to learn each new dance as soon as it was introduced at the court.

New dances were introduced often enough. With balls so popular and so frequent, it was easy to tire of the old ones. Something different was always welcome.

At first many of the new dances were created for the pleasure of the guests at a tournament. Sometimes it was for the ball, which almost always ended the festivities. Sometimes it was as part of the procession or the pageant, which followed the jousting match. It was during these ceremonies that the loveliest of all the ladies present bestowed the prizes on the bravest of the knights. In either case, the new dance was bound to mimic a battle.

But many other dances—not just those created for tournaments—also imitated battles. In some the knights and nobles brandished real weapons. In others they merely suggested swordplay by their movements.

Gradually, though, they stopped imitating swordplay. Instead they made swordplay's methods—or those of fencing—part of dance itself. They stood the way fencers stood. They adopted their positions. And they used many of the movements of dueling in dance.

They had learned these techniques of fencing, of dueling, at their daily lessons. And they learned them well. Every noble, every knight, knew that his very life depended on his skill with his rapier.

The first thing he was taught was to "center his weight"—to place it at the very center of his body. When he did, he formed a kind of axis—almost like the stem of a flower—down the middle of it. As long as the courtier kept his weight on that axis, he kept his balance, too.

That axis was the point where all the fencer's movements began. And how quick those movements were! With no weight in his arms or legs—with his weight at the center of his body—his arms and legs, his hands and feet, were as light as air. Because his arms were so light, the courtier moved them freely, in great sweeping circles.

The size of those circles gave him greater reach. Parrying an opponent, he could catch him wherever he wanted to. He was not limited to a narrow target as he was when he held a heavy sword or a long lance. Instead, his target was very broad.

At the same time, the courtier moved his arms freely, he balanced them carefully. If his body was like the stem of a plant, his arms were like two leaves, one on each side. And when he moved one arm with—or against—the other, he steadied himself even more.

That center—that axis—was important. But a fencer must also have a base to stand on. Just as a plant must have roots deep in the earth, a fencer must have his feet planted squarely on the ground. His fencing master showed him how to turn his feet out. That was not new. As a noble—as a courtier—he had been doing that all his life, just to appear elegant. But now he had to turn them out even farther, to keep his stance. And so he did.

Keeping his balance—steadying himself—standing with his feet planted firmly on the ground was all well and good. But standing still was hardly the point of fencing. Moving —and moving with what seemed the speed of light—was what the fencer must do.

And so his fencing master taught him to poise himself on the ball of the foot, keeping each of them turned out all the while. From there—from the ball of the foot—the courtier could move in any direction and in the fraction of a second. He could lunge forward. He could pull away. He could step aside. And he could do it instantly.

But the courtier must be strong, too. Riding had already given him muscles—in his thighs—that were like bands of coiled steel. When he crouched—something else his fencing master taught him to do—he was ready to spring forward with the speed of a pouncing tiger.

All this the courtier learned from his fencing master. And he soon saw that it would serve him as well at a ball as it did in a duel.

If he turned his feet out when he danced, he gave himself a firm base. Once he had that, he would not be thrown off balance, no matter what the position of his head or arms or shoulders. If he bent his knees he could leap in the air, crossing his feet or beating one against the other.

If he centered his weight, his arms were free; he could do what he wanted with them. His feet were free, too; he could move them with a speed he had never known, and in the most complicated steps.

Once the courtier had depended on dance to make him an expert fencer. Now it was the other way around. The courtier depended on fencing to make him an expert dancer.

A French monk, Thoinot Arbeau, showed how important fencing was to dance in a book published in 1588. The book was called *Orchésographie* and was one of the first on dance ever written.

In it a young man named Capriol asks how he can "acquire the art of dancing." He is told that it "will be an easy thing to acquire by the reading of French books to sharpen your wits and by the practice of sword-play."

And Arbeau has advice on the way he is to move. "When I speak of going straight forward, I mean not to turn the body entirely, because you will dance with a good grace if you present first your right, then your left side to the damsel, as if you wished to fence."

Capriol learns quickly. And why shouldn't he, since, as he puts it, "Sword play already taught me all those gestures?"

WHAT THE FRENCH COURTIERS—the lords and the nobles—learned when they traveled also became part of what is now ballet.

Travel was difficult in those days, but it was very popular. Nobles often journeyed about the countryside and stayed with other nobles in their castles. Sometimes they crossed borders, venturing into other countries. A wealthy lord might go as far away as Spain.

Wherever he went, he took his most trusted servants along. And his dancing master was always among them. The dancing master was closer to his lord than the others. Yet he was still a servant, although the noble might think of him more as a friend.

The lord asked his advice on many subjects, his opinion about many things. How should he dress for the evening's ball? Should he toast his host? If so, what should he say? And how should he respond if his host proposed a toast to him?

The lord might ask for advice in matters of love, too. How should he woo the beautiful maiden he saw at the window? First, though, would the dancing master learn

1400–1500. Nobles traveled and were entertained at banquets by those they visited.

who she was? Her name? Did she live in the castle? If she did, was she related to the baron? Was she his daughter, perhaps? His granddaughter? The lord insisted on knowing all this and more. Did she have other suitors? He was sure she did. (Who could resist falling in love with someone so charming, so lovely?) Finally, and most important. Had her hand, unluckily for him, already been promised in marriage?

If the answer was "no," the dancing master urged his lord to send a message to the lady. A letter, swearing his undying love. A poem.

The dancing master often helped his lord write the missive. And the lord certainly asked him to deliver it to the lady. Later, he questioned his messenger closely.

Was the lady pleased? Did she smile? Frown? Was it possible that she had blushed? The noble must know. And the dancing master must tell him. He held a special place in the noble's household and that was one of his duties.

People looked up to him for his manners and copied them, too. At every castle and court, the dancing master was the model for style and for taste.

When a nobleman visited the castle of another, he was lavishly entertained. A banquet was prepared in his honor; a hunt was arranged. And a ball was sure to be given.

At that ball, the dancing master was at the side of his lord. If a new dance was performed, he watched it carefully. And before they set out on their return journey, he knew all the steps.

Once home, word spread quickly that the lord had brought back a new dance. Those courtiers who had remained behind soon learned it, too. And in no time at all, everyone in the castle—and the region around it—knew that dance.

THE PAVANE was brought back from Spain and was slow and stately. It took its name from the Spanish word *pavo* which means peacock. And those who danced the pavane posed and preened and postured, just like that gorgeous—and foolish—bird.

To dance a pavane, everyone formed a circle. And they took such tiny steps that it seemed they only stepped forward and back, forward and back.

They had great dignity, though, and so the dance became a favorite. It was so well-liked that it was almost always the first dance at any great ball.

The dance that followed the pavane at such a ball was usually the galliard. It came from Italy, where "galliarde" once meant a gay and dashing person.

There was much jumping and leaping in the galliard. And it was also very fast. Sometimes dancers seemed to race across the floor.

It too was a great favorite. Still, some people were shocked by it. There were even those who called it shameful and said it was "an invention of the devil."

The sarabande was also a favorite at the French courts. Like the pavane, it came from Spain. It was never a peasant dance, though, like the pavane. Instead, it had begun as part of a church ceremony and so was very slow and very solemn, too.

As time passed, the sarabande lost its religious meaning. But for centuries after, it was performed at courts and castles all through Europe. Because it came from Spain, dancers often clacked castanets in time to the music of the sarabande.

Nobles who visited Germany came back with still another dance. It was called the allemande—the French word that means German. It was also slow and stately.

Through the years, as styles and tastes changed, people grew tired of the pavane. In its place they danced the newer allemande. Soon that was the dance most often chosen to open a ball.

Just as the courtiers tired of the pavane, they grew tired of the galliard. The more fashionable preferred a new dance from Italy. It was called the courante.

The courante was very fast, as fast as the galliard. Those who danced it took tiny, running steps, or glided across the floor. As they did, they flirted with each other. That was part of the dance itself.

All well-educated and well-mannered men—that is, all gentlemen—and their ladies knew other dances, too. Some, which had only been danced by peasants before, were as gay and lively as ever when they were danced in the castles.

One of the liveliest of all was the gigue. It was popular everywhere; it was danced in every country in Europe. It is still danced in many countries. Now, though, it is called "jig," and not "gigue." But music for it is still played on a violin—on a fiddle.

Just as each lord or lady knew the steps of each dance, each knew the order in which the dances were performed. That order was the same in every castle, in every court.

The first dance was slow and stately. With its pomp and majesty, it was a very formal ceremony. When the ceremony was over, everyone relaxed. Then they danced something very fast and very joyful.

A slow dance came next so that everybody could catch their breath. When all had rested, the musicians played another fast dance.

Each new dance, though, brought more than just the change from fast to slow, from slow to fast. It brought a change of accent, of beat; it brought a change of rhythm.

Such changes added a great deal of interest to the dances. And it added so much interest to the music that composers began to write dance music which was meant only to be heard.

In this music, they used the rhythms of the popular dances. And they arranged their pieces in the order of the dances at a ball. Slow, fast, slow, fast. Allemande, courante, sarabande, gigue.

Pieces of music arranged in this way are known as a "suite." The word is French; it means "something that follows." That was just what those pieces did; one followed the other in a definite order. Some composers still write suites. Often, though, they add two more dances—or "movements"—as they are called in music.

Many composers write other music also in four movements—slow, fast, slow fast. Some write it in three movements, but always with the same change of tempo. When this music is written for a single instrument—or for two— it is called a "sonata." When it is written for an orchestra, it is called a "symphony." But whatever it is called, it still follows the order of dances at balls held in great castles hundreds of years ago. It follows the order that gave the nobles—lords and ladies—a chance to catch their breath.

V

FRENCH NOBLES traveled to many lands. And nobles from those lands traveled to France. Each learned a great deal from the other; each taught the other a great deal. But perhaps no one taught the French so much as a young Italian princess.

Her name was Catherine de Medici, and she went to France to live, not just to visit.

Catherine was born in 1517, a little more than a hundred years after the Battle of Agincourt. Her birthplace was what is now the city of Florence, in what is now the country of Italy.

At that time, though, Italy was not yet a nation. And Florence was really a small country, or city-state. There were many in Italy at the time, but of them all, Florence was the richest.

Her citizens were prosperous. Some were even very wealthy. Florence, though, was rich in something more important than gold. Florence was rich in culture.

The city was filled with great art treasures—marvelous paintings and statues. Its libraries contained many books. And Florence was the home of scores of writers and poets and musicians, too. Their names and works would be known for hundreds of years.

All this splendor was due to the genius of Catherine's great-grandfather. His name was Lorenzo de Medici. He was better known, though, as "Lorenzo the Magnificent."

As the ruler of Florence, Lorenzo had great power. He also had great wealth. That wealth was measured in gold and silver and jewels—in rich and beautiful cloth. In rare spices, and in every imaginable treasure.

Lorenzo's palace was immense, and as beautiful as any. He had scores of servants at his command. He had hundreds of courtiers at his call. But it was not this splendor that gave Lorenzo his name. He was called "the Magnificent" because of his wealth of ideas. He was called "the Magnificent" because he was so generous to men of genius.

Lorenzo paid the architects who designed the wonderful buildings of Florence from his own pocket. He paid the painters and sculptors who decorated them, too. He spent his own fortune on the universities he founded and for the books that filled the libraries.

Lorenzo rewarded poets and writers with bags of gold. And, for all the citizens of Florence, he staged plays and processions and pageants. Dance was as much a part of them as it was part of the processions and pageants that followed the jousting matches. And, like Lorenzo's name, all were "magnificent."

Catherine loved beauty as much as Lorenzo did. And she was just as generous to artists in France as he had been to artists in Italy. She too ordered plays and pageants staged, ones that far outshone anything Lorenzo had dreamed of. But only the nobility would see them—not the other, ordinary people of France.

Catherine was only fourteen when she was engaged to the son of the French king, Francis I. She was fifteen when she was married. Her husband, Henry, Duke of Orléans, was sixteen years old.

The wedding took place in France, in the city of Marseilles. When Catherine sailed into the harbor there, one fine October day, she was on board the first of a fleet of more than sixty ships.

Catherine's ship had sails of purple cloth, embroidered with gold. The ship of her uncle, Pope Clement, was close behind. Its deck was covered with crimson satin. Above the deck was a tent of cloth of gold, to shield him from the sun.

Except for her uncle, who would perform the wedding ceremony, there were few relatives with Catherine on her voyage. She had been an orphan from the time she was very young and had almost none.

Instead of family, most of the other ships carried household goods—linens and silver and furniture—of great beauty and luxury. They carried the gifts offered to Catherine to honor her coming marriage, too. Other ships carried Catherine's household staff and servants. Her cooks were among them. They brought the secrets of Italian cooking and taught them to the French. Soon exotic new dishes appeared on the tables of the French nobles.

Catherine brought musicians with her, too, and actors and dancers. And she brought her own dancing master as well. All had had the finest training. All served Catherine well in her new land.

It was the duty of Catherine's household staff to stage the festivities of the court. Sometimes these celebrations honored a member of the royal family of France. Some-

1519–1589.
Catherine de Medici,
the French queen,
planned
magnificent
entertainments for
visiting royalty.

times they honored the king or queen of another country. In any case, the great banquets, the plays and pageants that entertained her guests were magnificent. And that was just as it should be for a descendent of a ruler known as "the Magnificent."

Not only were Catherine's entertainments as splendid as those of her great-grandfather, they were also, and in many ways, very much like them.

The entertainments arranged for Lorenzo in the Medici palace in Florence centered around a grand dinner. Often the dinner lasted four or five hours.

The most delicious food was served at them. Very often, it was set before the guests in strange and wondrous ways. Roast peacock—and roast pheasant—wore their own bright tail feathers as decoration. Their beady eyes peered from their small, brightly colored heads. Tiny live birds were tucked beneath the crusts of meat pies. When the pies were opened—it was like the nursery rhyme—the birds soared off to the ceiling. Sometimes the food was formed in the shape of a swan or a deer, sometimes like a person or an animal from some ancient myth.

No one went hungry at such a meal, where course followed course, one after the other. Fish and fowl and meat. Wild game and wild birds. Soups and sauces. Breads and pastries. Pies and cakes and cheeses. The fruits of the season, peaches or apples or grapes or oranges, all piled high on silver platters. Desserts of every type, even ice cream, were passed. The choicest wines were poured from silver or gold flasks and pitchers.

One course followed another. But between them the guests were delighted by dozens of different entertainers. Actors performed scenes from plays. Poets recited verses. Musicians sang or strummed on lutes or viols. And dancers moved gracefully as they presented a story—like the scenes played by the actors—from some ancient myth.

They performed at one end of the banquet hall, where a model of a building of some sort was set up. Sometimes it was a tower; more often it was a bridge. Although it was only made of *papier-mâché*—pressed paper—it was built with such skill that it almost looked real. White clouds hung above the bridge or tower. And some of the entertainers floated down on them to enter the hall.

Once those who entertained at balls and banquets were troubadours, wandering from one castle to another. If they stayed at them, it was only for a few days. But by the time of Lorenzo, they were no longer traveling players. Instead, each spent his whole life at the court where he performed.

They were not courtiers, however. Like the cooks

who prepared the meal—and like the dancing masters—they were really servants. Some were treated very well. But others were treated only a little better than the kitchen help. Yet among those poets and painters and composers were artists who created works that are still admired.

Poems and plays and dances that were performed between the courses of the dinners were given a French name, "*entremets*," or in Italian, "*intermezzi*." Both words were taken from two Latin words. One of them literally meant "between." The literal meaning of the other was "food placed on the table." Put together, they meant "between the courses of a meal." Each was as fanciful as the food served the guests. And each suggested what that course would be.

Had the cooks prepared wild boar? The dancers interpreted a hunting scene. Fish? For that there were songs about a brook or stream. Fruit? What better than a dancer dressed as the goddess of the harvest?

Entertainment—and dance—were very much part of a great banquet. And so some of the words used to describe them are now seen on menus. Because each of the *entremets* was followed by a new dish, certain courses of a meal are still called "*entrées*," meaning "entrance" in French, now referring to the dish itself, not just the serving of it. And today, in France, an *entremets* is the dish served between the roast and the dessert.

From the time of Lorenzo, banquets of this sort were the custom in Italy. The custom had already spread to France, even before the arrival of Catherine.

But never did the French see such splendid affairs as those given by—or for—Catherine de Medici. The most splendid of all were the royal weddings.

VI

THE FIRST ROYAL WEDDING was that of Catherine and Henry, the duke of Orléans. All Marseilles was decked out in splendor for it. Flags fluttered from every house. Panels of silk and velvet hung from every balcony. Many were embroidered with gold or silver. When the threads of precious metal caught the sun, the whole city seemed on fire.

The palaces of the pope and the king were just as lavishly decorated as the city. They stood opposite one another, with a wide street between them. Each was bright with banners. Each was strung with pennants.

A covered bridge was built over that street, for the balls and banquets held in honor of the young couple. The bridge linked the palaces and formed a huge hall. It, too, was beautifully decorated, with costly tapestries and hangings.

A full month of festivities passed before Catherine and her young husband, Henry, set out for Paris. They made the journey on horseback. And the entire French court went with them.

That court was made up of the King, Francis I, and

his sister, along with other close relatives—aunts and uncles, nephews and nieces, cousins once or twice removed. There were hundreds of nobles, and courtiers beyond counting.

And there were members of the clergy—men of the church. The most important was the Pope, Clement. He, though, would only go as far as Avignon. But the others, from bishops and cardinals down to simple friars and abbots, went all the way to Paris.

The king had his counselors with him. He had his ministers. He had advisers and guards and soldiers. He had a huge household staff as well. His favorite cooks, his most gifted pastry chefs. He had brought them from Paris and now he must take them back. There were actors and musicians. There were dancers. The king's dancing master went along. And his fencing master, too.

Besides the king's servants, there were those who came from Florence with Catherine. And there were her own linens and silver and gold. All were part of that long procession that wound its way north to Paris.

Francis I loved to ride and he loved to hunt. In all of France there was no better place for such sports than in the Loire Valley. The king owned many marvelous *chateaux*, castles, in this valley, and spent most of his time there. He moved from one castle to another, rarely spending more than two weeks in each at a time.

Often Catherine, who liked to ride and to hunt almost as much as her father-in-law, went with Francis. She was almost as expert as he.

Francis and Catherine shared a great interest in learning, too. And Catherine was both witty and wise. If she had not been, Francis would hardly have noticed her. Henry, her husband, was only the second son of the king.

And in France at that time, neither the second son—whether of king or noble or land-owning knight—nor the wife of a second son counted for much.

But Francis admired Catherine. He liked the ideas she brought from Florence. So he did not ask her to adopt French customs; instead he adopted many Italian ones. And since everyone copied the king, those ideas spread through the land.

When Catherine and Henry had been married three years, the king's older son died. And Henry, who had been only a duke, became the dauphin, the crown prince. He would be king someday; Catherine would be queen.

That day came after eleven years. When her husband was crowned as Henry II of France, Catherine de Medici was at his side. She did not rule France; that was the king's duty. Catherine's duty was to bring up her children and to educate them properly. But, like King Francis and like Lorenzo de Medici, too, she also devoted her time to music and literature, to science. And to dance.

More palaces were built; Catherine chose the architects who designed them. She hired sculptors to carve the statues that decorated them. She hired landscape experts who planned the marvelous gardens around them. She hired artists and craftsmen and paid them to create the masterpieces they longed to. She did the same for poets and playwrights and writers. Catherine collected the finest examples of the crafts of her day—tapestries, enamels, jewelry, china, rare books. She gave wonderful concerts. And

The splendor and elegance of this royal wedding celebration
was typical of the courts of Catherine de Medici and of Louis XIV.

whenever the occasion arose—a royal birthday, a christening, a victory on the battlefield or a visit from afar—she arranged the banquets and entertainments. The most exciting of the entertainments celebrated the weddings of members of Catherine's family. There were three such weddings in just one year.

The first was that of Catherine's eldest son, Francis, and Mary, Queen of Scots. The ceremony took place in the most sacred of all French cathedrals, Notre-Dame in Paris. Later there was a great ball. It was held in a palace just across the Seine River.

The ball began with a parade of coaches around the hall. They were drawn by pairs of marvelous mechanical horses.

The horses' backs were draped with velvet cloths; their harnesses were of gold and silver, studded with jewels. Their trappings were just like those of the horses spurred into battle at Agincourt. And they were ridden by young and graceful Dukes of France. Just like those who fought at Agincourt.

The horses drew carriages crowded with splendidly costumed pilgrims. They were followed by six ships, each covered with crimson velvet. As they sailed around the room, they tossed back and forth on the waves of a mechanical sea.

The bride and groom rode in the first ship; the king and queen rode in the second. And nobles of the highest rank rode in the other four. All wore beautiful costumes. And they wore brilliant jewels which shimmered in the light of thousands of candles.

The second wedding was that of Henry's sister. It was just as impressive as the first. And like Catherine's own—

and that of her son—the festivities went on for days.

The last wedding was the wedding of Catherine's eldest daughter. Because it was so special, it ended with a real tournament. And the king himself was to take part in it.

Catherine's astrologer, though, warned against this. And Catherine too urged Henry not to joust. Nevertheless, Henry rode into the lists. Like a knight of old—and true to the traditions of chivalry—he swore to win for love of Catherine.

Henry held his long lance before him and lunged at his opponent. The two clashed, with a great clatter and a terrible sound. Suddenly the sharp metal point of his foe's lance slid through the king's visor. It struck him in the eye.

He fell to the ground, unconscious. And ten days later, Henry II was dead.

VII

THERE WERE TERRIBLE DAYS ahead for Catherine. She loved her husband deeply. To mourn him, she wore widow's weeds—somber black clothing—for the rest of her life.

But there was a new king now. He was Catherine's eldest son. And Catherine was no longer Queen. Instead, her title was Queen Mother. Because the new King, Francis II, was just a child, Catherine's duties were much the same. Life at court went on, just as it had before. Once again, Catherine was at its center. She still loved to ride and to hunt. And she still loved to dance. She never gave up these pleasures.

Catherine still spent much time adding to her fine collections of china and books and tapestries. She still befriended artists, giving them large sums of money so that they were free to write or paint or compose. And she still arranged the marvelous banquets and balls she was famous for.

Any happy event was reason for some such entertainment. And the one given for the visiting ambassadors from Poland was brilliant. Their mission, too, was a happy one.

They came to offer the Polish crown to Catherine's third son, Henry. In return, Catherine honored them with a lavish spectacle. It was staged by an Italian dancing master who had recently arrived in France. And, as was the custom, it combined processions and pageants, poetry and music. And dance.

It was as beautiful—as stunning—as any seen so far. The costumes were splendid. The scenery was breathtaking. As the dance began, sixteen beautiful young girls stood atop a rock. That rock, with the help of mysterious machinery, glided all around the room.

Music was especially written for the dance. It was as lovely as any had ever heard. Yet it was not for the music or the scenery or the costumes that people from one end of the land to the other remembered the ballet. It was because of the dance itself. It was because, as they performed, the sixteen young girls all moved as one.

They went through the most difficult and complicated steps. They jumped up, each beating her feet together. They turned—all at the same time. They twirled—all at the same time. No one had ever seen anything like it. And no one would forget it. They talked of it for many, many years.

Splendid though it was, the entertainment was not nearly so lavish as that given at Catherine's court a few years later. This was to honor Catherine's daughter-in-law, who was now Queen of France. But, although it honored the Queen, it celebrated the wedding of the Queen's sister.

It was not an important wedding. The Queen's sister was not of high rank, and neither was her husband-to-be. But Catherine wanted an excuse to show the world her wealth. The wedding gave it to her.

She asked one of her most trusted aides to plan the entertainment. Like Catherine, he was Italian. But he changed his name to make it sound more like a French name, and so he was called Balthasar de Beaujoyeulx.

Balthasar was Catherine's *valet-de-chambre*—the head of her whole household staff. But he was much more. He was the chief violinist at the court, too. And he was Catherine's own dancing master.

The men under Beaujoyeulx's command were as talented as he was. And he set them to work for him. The court poet wrote verses. One court composer wrote songs. A second court composer wrote music for different instruments—for flutes and violins.

A painter designed scenery. An engineer designed floats. Balthasar himself arranged the dances. Moreover, he supervised everything. And before he was through, he had spent many hundreds of thousands of dollars of Catherine's money.

The wedding—with its festivities—took place at Fontainebleau, near Paris. It was one of the largest and most beautiful of all the royal palaces. And it was surrounded by a vast and lovely park.

More than ten thousand people were invited to the great celebration. Thousands more came, hoping to catch a glimpse of the festivities. Most, though, could do nothing but roam through the park. Only the luckiest got close enough to the palace to peer through the windows.

Those who did saw a canopy erected at one end of a long, long hall. Beneath it were the seats for the royal family.

To one side of those seats was a grassy nook. It was the home of Pan, the Greek god of field and forest. At the

1581. A wedding at Fontainebleau, her largest and most beautiful castle, displayed Catherine de Medici's wealth.

center of the nook was a grotto—a deep cave. Within it lay pools of limpid blue water. The nook itself glowed with the light from candles and lanterns placed in the trees that surrounded it.

On the other side of the place reserved for the royal family was a golden vault—a huge, gilded shell—where the musicians sat. That too was bright with light. And so were the white clouds that floated above their heads.

A castle stood at the far end of the hall, opposite the King and Queen. It was built of papier-mâché, and there was a garden around it. That castle was supposed to be the home of Circe. And—in legend—Circe was the enchantress who turned men into animals.

As night fell, the most important of the invited guests entered the hall. Almost all stood—either on the floor of the hall or on raised platforms—along the walls. Only a few, aside from the royal family, could be seated. When they finally took their places, the entertainment began.

It started with an overture. When the music ended, a man dressed in cloth of silver dashed from Circe's palace into the hall. He was a gentleman-in-waiting to Catherine, but for this evening he was a poor mortal changed by Circe into a lion, then back into a mortal.

He ran to the king, terrified. He begged his help. Circe, he said, would turn him into an animal again.

Just then Circe herself burst from the castle. She was furious because she had let a human being escape her power. It would not be for long, she vowed. And then she went back to her castle.

The doors closed behind her and a group of dancers entered the hall. Like Circe, they were figures from ancient mythology.

Some—the Tritons—had the heads and shoulders of men. But they were half fish, too, with fish tails—marvelous costumes covered with scales of gold and silver, which they draped over their arms.

Others—the Sirens—were half bird, half woman. Their costumes were covered with brightly-colored feathers.

A dozen violinists followed. They wore suits of gleaming satin, trimmed with gold. Then came pages, dressed in equal splendor. After the pages, a marvelous float was drawn through the hall.

Jets of water sprayed from the fountain in the center of the float. And many of the most noble ladies in all of France sat on golden steps around it. They were dressed as nymphs and naiads—beautiful maidens who lived in the woods.

Around and around the procession went. And how it pleased the guests! At last, though, the Tritons and the Sirens, along with the rest of the procession left the hall. Then the nymphs and the naiads stepped down from the float for the first dance of the ballet.

Balthasar had a French name for the procession. He called it an *interméde*. The name is still used at times. More often, though, the Italian word *intermezzo* is used. It had been used, with a slightly different spelling, at the court of Lorenzo de Medici. And it had the same meaning as the French word *entremets*, between the courses of a meal.

As time passed, the meaning of *intermezzo* lost its connection with food. It was used now in connection with entertainment. And it meant an entertainment of one kind introduced into an entertainment of another kind.

For Balthasar, it meant the processions and parades and pageantry which came between two sets of dances. And for him, *entrée* meant the dances themselves, not the entrance of dishes at a banquet.

Entremets—or *intermezzo*—or *interméde*, with the *entrée* following. Balthasar took the banquets of Florence a hundred years earlier as the pattern for his ballet. It would be the pattern for ballet for a hundred years to come.

And he drew on the entire court for his performers. Not only did he press into service the composers and musicians and painters and poets; he brought in gentlemen and courtiers, lords and ladies. He brought members of the nobility in to dance and to act.

Like the feasts at the Medici Palace, the ballet at Fontainebleau continued for many hours. It began at ten at night; it was nearly four in the morning before it ended. But during all that time, the other lords and ladies, the royal guests, the important people—the most important in France or even all Europe—watched spellbound as the story of Circe unfolded.

The man Circe had bewitched and turned into a lion had been turned back into a mortal. But he still feared her. Hadn't she made it plain that she would work her magic on him again, turning him back into a lion? Hadn't she proved her powers by casting a spell over the dancing nymphs, turning them to stone?

The nymphs were saved, though, by Mercury, the messenger of the gods, floating down from the heavens on a cloud. Mercury freed the nymphs and they danced again. There was another *intermède* then, with a group of satyrs —woodland creatures with the heads of men and the bodies of goats—roaming through the hall and singing.

More chariots and floats rolled through the hall. They carried still more dancers. The last was drawn by a mon-

Satyrs—*mythical creatures with the heads of men and the bodies of goats—roamed the hall as part of* The Comic Ballet of Queen Louise.

strous serpent. Pallas Athena, the goddess of wisdom, rode atop it. She asked Jupiter, the god who ruled all people and all other gods, too, for his help. He appeared at once, riding on an eagle. Thunder rolled then and lightning flashed across the sky. And Jupiter himself led an attack on the castle of Circe. After it was captured—and Circe killed by another of Jupiter's thunderbolts—all the gods and goddesses who had appeared so far came back for what seemed to be a final dance.

But it was not quite that. Because then, almost all those who had watched the ballet moved onto the floor of the hall. And there they joined the performers in sarabandes and pavanes, in courantes and gigues—in all the dances they loved so much.

WHAT A TRIUMPH that night was for Catherine de Medici! As she had hoped, her wealth was displayed to all the world.

And what a triumph it was for Balthasar, Catherine's *valet-de-chambre*. He had shown the world his genius. He did so by creating the first real ballet ever. That was in 1581, more than four hundred years ago.

That ballet is no longer performed; most of the directions for it were lost centuries ago. But its name lives on. *Ballet Comique de la Reine Louise*. The Comic Ballet of Queen Louise.

The ballet was called "comic" only because it was not tragic, because it had a happy ending. And, although it was created at Catherine's bidding, it honored her daughter-in-law. And so her name, Queen Louise, was given to it.

And ballet? The name came from an Italian word, "balletto." It means "little dance." Ballet was not called "little," though, because it was short or because it lacked importance. Ballet was given its name because in Italy people often use the word "little" as a sign of affection. A ballet—a "little dance"—was something very special.

The French, like the Italians, considered dance very special. They considered the ballet for Queen Louise even more special because it seemed so new. Yet all parts of the ballet were really very old.

The battles in it were like tournaments and jousting matches. The dances were like those of the courtiers at balls at the palaces. And parades and pageants and poetry —pantomime and plays—had entertained the nobility for as long as anyone could remember.

The story of Circe had been told over and over. Great splendor, too, had been the style since the time of Lorenzo the Magnificent. And Lorenzo's banquets had even been the model for Balthasar's ballet.

In almost every way, the new entertainment was like many that had come before. But it was different in one very important way. It was different because one single idea ran through the whole ballet. And everything in the ballet was in keeping with that idea.

If dancers were dressed as Tritons—or Sirens—or goddesses of any sort, it was because there were Tritons or Sirens or goddesses in the story. They wore costumes that were suitable.

The scenery was exactly right for the play. The music was right. The songs and the verses and the dances, too.

Everything in the ballet belonged in it. Even the *intermédes*, the floats, the battles. They belonged because they served the same purpose. That purpose was to tell the story of Circe.

Because Balthasar succeeded so well, he was hailed everywhere for his talent. The final dance was hardly over before word of his triumph was on everybody's lips.

A book was published that described all the steps of

the ballet. The music for it was printed, too. And so were the verses. That book sold far and wide, not only in France and England, but in all the countries of Europe.

Nobles who heard of the new ballet wanted to put them on—and at once—at their own courts. And soon ballets were seen everywhere.

At a very large court, headed by a powerful king or noble, a great deal of money was spent for costumes and scenery. The ballet must be as splendid as the king—or prince—or lord could afford. But no one could afford a ballet as magnificent as that given in honor of Queen Louise.

Catherine de Medici had spent a huge fortune on that ballet. And though she was willing to pay the bills for it, there was little money in the state treasury for her to draw on. All too often, the money to pay for the ballet was borrowed. Just as often, other bills were not paid at all.

Catherine really could not afford that first ballet. She certainly could not afford another like it. Because besides an empty treasury France faced other problems.

She was at war with many of her neighbors and could not pay for those wars. Moreover, there were frightful religious wars right at home. During these, Frenchmen fought other Frenchmen over the way each should worship. Because of this, a terrible massacre took place; there was terror throughout the land.

The King, Henry III, who returned from Poland to rule his own country after the deaths of both Francis II and Charles IX, was a strange person who was very much disliked. After the death of Catherine—a few years after the ballet was given—he became still more unpopular. Because he had no heir—even his younger brother, Catherine's last son, was dead—fighting broke out among those who wanted the throne.

Henry, who was both cruel and weak, had some of his foes assassinated. Because of such acts, many more of his subjects turned against him. He was forced to leave Paris and flee to Tours, one of his castles in the Loire Valley. When he returned to Paris, he was stabbed to death by a monk.

Henry of Navarre, a cousin of Henry III, became king of France then. Known as Henry IV, he was as different from Henry III as heat is from cold. The French still think of him as one of their greatest rulers.

Henry brought peace to the land. With peace there was time for pleasure again. The nobles no longer spent their time fighting; they no longer lived in fear. And soon all the splendor of the courts was restored.

The new king, like Catherine before him, employed artists of all sorts. Other nobles followed his example. They gave sumptuous banquets. And they entertained at balls and ballets. More than eighty ballets were presented at the court of Henry IV alone. But Henry IV's life ended tragically, and much too soon: he was assassinated by a madman. Because he was so well loved by his people, all mourned him.

Henry's son, Louis XIII, enjoyed ballet as much as his father had, and many were created for his court while he ruled France. King Louis often danced in those ballets himself. Sometimes he even took a leading part. And sometimes he wrote the music for the ballets, too.

Most of those who danced in the court ballets were, like King Louis, amateurs. They were courtiers who danced only because they enjoyed it, and not because they were paid to. But there were others who were not ama-

1625. That first ballet of Catherine de Medici's led to many others. Here is a scene from one, Les Feés des Forêt de Sainte-Germaine (*The Fairies of the Forest of St. Germain*).

teurs, but professionals. Dancing was their job; it was how they earned a living.

Many were dancing masters. Others were gifted pupils who would some day teach. They spent far more of their time at practice or in rehearsal than the courtiers. And because they were so much better trained, they could perform much more difficult steps.

Such professional dancers were always men. The ladies of the court appeared only in ballets that were private entertainments. There they danced for their own amusement. When an audience was present to watch a formal ballet, the roles of women were taken by young boys wearing wigs and masks.

But when the ballet was over—when the story had

been told—those who took part joined the ladies—and the other lords—in the center of the hall. And there everyone danced. Their steps, though, were not those difficult ones of the ballet. They were the simpler steps of the social dances, of the court dances. What took place in the center of the hall was not ballet, but a court ball.

Often neither the ballet nor the ball that followed was enough to satisfy King Louis and his courtiers. So they left his palace and went on to another palace. And at that other palace, they repeated the same ballet they had danced earlier.

Even that, though, did not always satisfy the group. Nothing satisfied them until all had made their way to the town hall. And on a platform in the square in front of it they performed the same ballet still another time. Now, though, it was for the pleasure of the people of the town, rather than the courtiers, the nobility.

But when the ballet ended, the nobles and courtiers—and even the king—stepped down from the platform and joined the crowd that had watched them dance. And still another ball took place, just as one did after a ballet in a palace.

IX

NO EARLIER FRENCH RULER—not Catherine or Henry or Louis XIII—loved ballet as much as Louis XIV did. And no one did so much to make it great.

In 1643, when he was only five years old, Louis XIV became King of France. He was far too young to rule himself, so his mother, with the help of ministers and counselors, ruled for him. But from the day of his birth, Louis was trained to behave like a monarch. And the best teachers, not only in France but all Europe, were brought to court to teach the boy.

Even when he was young, Louis XIV was an excellent dancer. When he was only fourteen, he took a leading role in a ballet given at his own court. That ballet lasted thirteen hours. It was called the *Ballet de la Nuit—* The Ballet of the Night.

The role that Louis danced was that of Apollo. And in ancient myths, Apollo was the Sun King. So the young French King wore a costume as bright as the sun in the heavens. A golden sun was stitched to the front of his costume, and sunbeams were hung around his neck, on his shoulders, around his wrists and his knees. He even wore small suns on his shoes. Because of that role in that ballet,

*1653. Louis XIV was fourteen when he played the sun in a
court ballet. He has been called "The Sun King" ever since.*

Louis XIV is still known as *Le Roi Soleil*—"The Sun King."

Every day, for more than twenty years, King Louis had a lesson with his dancing master. And he enjoyed dancing until the end of his life. But as he grew older, Louis XIV also grew heavier. He no longer moved easily or gracefully. And he could no longer perform difficult steps. So then he only danced at balls; he no longer danced in ballets.

As Louis grew older, affairs of state kept him busy, too. He still was surrounded by ministers and counselors. The power was no longer theirs, though, but his. Louis had been king of France for many years. Now he was the ruler of France as well. "The State—I am the State!" he proclaimed.

And what an important ruler he was! Louis was as powerful as any in Europe, perhaps as any in the world. His reign was one of such glory that it earned the King another name. He was called *Louis-le-Grand*—Louis the Great. He started industries. He encouraged trade. He expanded farming. And he supported the explorers who had gone to America. One, de la Salle, sailed down the Mississippi. He claimed the entire region for France. And he called it "Louisiana" for the King.

But above all, Louis XIV enjoyed life. He was surrounded by beautiful women. He lived in the greatest luxury. And his court was another marvel, even more glorious than that of Catherine de Medici or Francis I.

Although he no longer danced in ballet, Louis's interest in it never lessened. And though he no longer took dancing lessons himself, he still kept the finest teachers at his court. They taught the other nobles, and they created new ballets to amuse both the King and the court.

King Louis no longer lived in the immense palace in Paris, the Louvre, where he lived as a child. Instead, he held court at a palace in Versailles. It was closer to Paris than Fontainebleau. It was closer to Paris, too, than the magnificent *chateaux* of the Loire Valley. And it was safer than the Louvre. So he preferred Versailles to all the others.

The palace there was huge. Even so, it was not large enough for all the courtiers who followed Louis to it. So he added on—and on—and on to it. By the time it was finished, there was room there for five thousand people.

Even that was not large enough for all the nobles and courtiers—the lords and the ladies—who flocked to the side of the king. Five thousand more had to be housed in the villages nearby.

Almost all these people owned palaces, too. They had their own farms and forests and estates, but they had to let stewards manage their business affairs—although many would have liked to manage them themselves. If they did not live at the court, and leave business matters to their stewards, the king would not grant them favors. Worse, he might increase their taxes. He certainly would not appoint their sons to government posts. It was clearly in their own best interest to live at Versailles.

That was just what King Louis wanted. If they left court, they might think of their taxes, which always seemed to go up. They might object to the war he was waging. They might disapprove of this minister or of that policy. If the nobles and courtiers had good reason to stay at Versailles, the king had just as good reason to keep them there. And so he did.

One charming guest of the king, Madame de Sevigné,

1650–1700. Guests at the palace of Versailles enjoyed music, ballet and plays—and rides in gondolas and open carriages.

was famous for her letters. In one, she told of a day at Versailles. "At six we go riding in our *barouches*"—open carriages—"then we go out on the canal in gondolas. There music is being played; we return at ten and go to the play; midnight sounds and we take supper."

Music. Plays. Ballet. All were performed at Versailles. But new music, new plays, new ballets were always needed. So King Louis brought composers and playwrights and dancing masters to his court. Because he spared no expense, they were the finest in the world. Some—like the great writer Molière—were among the finest of all times.

Louis XIV brought architects to Versailles. They designed the many new wings of the palace and they designed scenery for plays and ballets, as well. He brought engineers to build that scenery—islands that sank beneath the sea, volcanoes that erupted in flames.

Although the nobles spent much of their time at Versailles, they returned to their homes from time to time. There, they entertained their own guests. They entertained them with balls. And with ballets. They copied the king in this, as they did in everything. But some began to make changes. There were new steps added, and some of those steps were not graceful. Sometimes jugglers or acrobats, even horses, performed alongside the dancers.

Such changes displeased King Louis. He believed that ballet should follow strict rules. So he ordered his dancing master, Pierre Beauchamps, to set them down. Those rules are followed to this day.

Beauchamps did more than set down the rules of ballet. He also listed all the steps dancers were permitted to use. They were the prettiest, the most graceful steps. Beauchamps would approve nothing else.

1602. Before Beauchamps described dance steps, artists pictured them. And before dancers used a practice barre *to steady themselves, they used a rope.*

After Beauchamps described the steps, he named them. Those names, too, are still used. Because Beauchamps was French, and in the service of a French king, all the names were French: *pas de chat*, or "cat's step;" *sissone*, or "scissor step;" *glissade*, or "glide." The language of ballet is still French.

Beauchamps also listed all the movements—not the steps, but the movements of ballet. Of these, by far the most important is the *plié*. The word means "bend." And that is what a dancer does in a *plié*. He bends his knees.

1650–1700. A noble, hands and feet in second position, follows the rules of the King's dancing master, Beauchamps.

After he listed the steps and the movements, Beauchamps listed the positions of ballet. He also numbered the basic arm and foot positions; the numbers—first position, second position, third, fourth, fifth—are still used, too.

In drawings to illustrate those positions, the feet are always turned out. Beauchamps was reminding dancers of what was sometimes forgotten; elegance is the soul of dance. He was reminding them that the elegance of king and courtier as they stood or walked came from the turned-out foot. And that that turnout made dance elegant, too.

He was also reminding them that dance was much like fencing. And that the turned-out foot that gave the

Academie pour les Armes tenue par le Sieur Motet rue de Seinë

1715. Three hundred years after Agincourt, gentlemen went to special schools for their daily fencing lessons.

courtier a steady base in one—and helped him keep his balance—gave him a steady base in the other.

Beauchamps made everything about ballet both clear and exact. So it was simple for those who came after him to teach dance. A ballet master no longer needed to explain a step or movement or position each time he wanted a student to perform it. Now he had a word—or a number —for it. Students quickly learned the meaning of each. And that was enough.

Once everyone understood the words and the numbers, there was a way to write down directions for a dance. So Beauchamps created a system of dance notation, much like notation for music. Because of this, ballets which might otherwise be forgotten are now remembered.

And Pierre Beauchamps is remembered, too. If it were not for him—and for his patron, King Louis XIV—ballet itself might be forgotten.

WHEN LOUIS XIV ordered Pierre Beauchamps to draw up rules for ballet, he took a giant step forward for dance. Then he took a second giant step. He founded a school for ballet.

The school was called The Royal Academy of the Dance. It was a national school, one for all in the country who showed great talent, great gifts. It was the first such school in the world. He set forth his reasons for founding the Royal Academy in a document called "The Letter Patent."

"The art of dancing," Louis said, was "one of the most suitable and necessary arts for physical development." It was important "for the most natural preparation of exercises concerning the use of weapons." And dance "is one of the most valuable and useful arts for nobles . . . not only in time of war in our armies . . . but even in time of peace in our ballets."

When the king spoke, everyone listened. So the nobles went on with their dancing lessons. And more ballets were created—and performed—than ever before. They were staged wherever there was a large, open space.

Sometimes that space was a banquet hall. Sometimes it was a ballroom. And very often, it was an indoor tennis court.

Ballets were performed outdoors, too. They were given on the lawns surrounding great castles. They were given in parks. They were performed on platforms set up at one end of the village or town or city square, opposite the village—or town—or city hall. At Versailles, though, ballets were performed in the stables.

Those stables were hardly ordinary stables. They were stables fit for the horses of one of the most powerful kings on earth and were far more comfortable than the huts of many of the peasants. The grooms and hands who cared for the king's horses often lived in bare and drafty hovels. Since the horses were considered far more valuable than the servants, they lived in bright, clean buildings.

Whatever the space, it was arranged like the great hall at Fontainebleau when the Ballet for Queen Louise was performed. The king sat at one end, on a raised dais, or platform. Others of the royal family, along with a few favored guests, sat beside or just behind him. The courtiers took their places along the sides. If the ballet was performed indoors, they leaned against the walls. Their ladies stood —or sometimes sat—among them. The scenery was set up at the far end, opposite the dais of the king. The ballet took place on the floor of the hall, in front of the papier-mâché towers and castles and bridges.

There was no need for a stage in the stables or the halls or the parks. Although the ballet was given in front of the scenery, it was near the center of the hall. The spectators were ranged around the dancers on three sides. Everyone could see them.

This floor plan, which worked so well for ballet

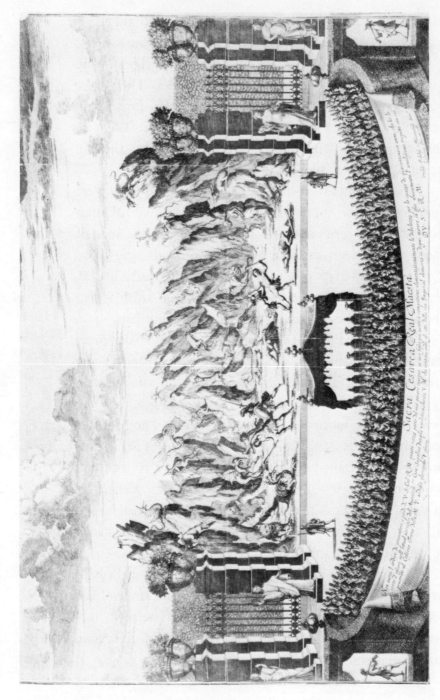

1660–1700. Ballets were often performed outdoors, sometimes in parks, sometimes on the lawns surrounding great castles.

worked just as well for concerts and for plays. And there were many of those at Versailles, too. King Louis had to entertain his guests in as many ways as possible to keep them there, no matter what the cost.

Louis XIV truly loved dance. But he loved music just as much. And so when he set up The Royal Academy of the Dance, he also set up The Royal Academy of Music. He chose an Italian composer who was a close friend to head it. The composer's name—changed to a French version—was Jean-Baptiste Lully.

Lully was only fourteen when he came to France. And just as Beaujoyeulx became *valet-de-chambre* to Catherine de Medici, Lully became *garçon-de-chambre* to the cousin of the king.

Garçon-de-chambre. Garçon, the French word for "boy." At fourteen, Lully was too young to be a *valet-de-chambre*. He was too young to manage a royal household. He was really only a page. But he was very close to the most important people at the court. He did his best to win their favor. Soon, Lully was a favorite at Versailles, almost a pet.

Lully was a graceful and elegant dancer. And so he danced at court ballets almost from the time he reached France. He even danced in the *Ballet de la Nuit*, where King Louis, no older than he, impressed all in the role of The Sun King.

When King Louis discovered that Lully was also a very fine musician, he established a small orchestra for him. And before long, he appointed him as his own music master. Louis respected Lully so much that when the musician was married, he and the queen were his witnesses.

Louis XIV was not only interested in dance and music.

1622–1673. Jean-Baptiste Molière, whose plays are still performed with ballets by Lully.

He was interested in theater, too. There were many troupes of players in France who wandered from one city to another, giving plays. And in Paris, the old tennis courts and ballrooms, where ballets and plays had been performed, were being converted into real theaters. They had stages and prosceniums—frames around the stages—much like theaters today.

One of these troupes was headed by the great Jean-Baptiste Molière. He not only wrote for the players, but directed them and acted, too. The king's brother, who was simply called *Monsieur*, or *Monsieur-le-Prince*, saw Molière's troupe in a city in the provinces. He liked it so much that he gave it the title of *Troupe de Monsieur*, and the right to use one of the new theaters in Paris.

Not much later, Molière and his troupe found favor with King Louis as well. To show his pleasure, he granted the company the title *Troupe de Roi*. Each year he gave them enough money to live on, and he took Molière to Versailles, to write plays for him.

Soon, Molière and Lully joined forces. And Lully began to create ballets for the Molière plays. These were not modeled on the great ballet of Balthasar; they did not advance the action of the play. Because they were simply slipped in between the acts, they were really *entremets* or *intermezzi* or *intermédes*. They were there to amuse the audience. But they had another purpose. They gave the actors a chance to change their costumes!

Instead of telling a story, these ballets merely depicted a single scene. And most often, it was of a feast. Dancers made their entrance on stage. Near the center of it, they set up an enormous banquet table. Other dancers entered with lighted candles in huge silver holders, which they placed on the tables. Still other dancers appeared. They paraded around the table carrying trays of food in the fanciest forms, the most marvelous shapes. Pheasants and peacocks, bright with feathers. Molded desserts that looked like small, shimmering towers. Silver platters piled high with glowing fruits. Except that the stage was small and the interlude brief—and that the food was made of plaster of Paris—it was just like one of Lorenzo's banquets at the Medici Palace.

Molière's band of actors found such favor with the king that he made them the Royal Troupe.

But Lully was not content just to compose music for plays someone else wrote. And so, as head of The Royal Academy of Music, he wrote operas—plays where the words are sung instead of spoken. And like Molière, he produced them, too.

It was Lully who arranged all the details of the performance. He chose the singers and he chose the designers. He selected costumes and directed the players, showing them where to move and when. Often, he conducted the orchestra, playing his own music.

Even that, though, was not enough for Jean-Baptiste Lully. He was so ambitious that he wanted to be director of The Academy of Dance as well as of The Academy of Music. He longed to take the place of Pierre Beauchamps. And because he was such a good friend of the king, he soon did. Beauchamps did not really mind. He was only interested in training dancers to move exactly according to his rules. He was not interested in new and daring ideas. Lully, though, had one such idea after another. And he was always eager to try them out.

One of his boldest was to stage ballets in a theater. And after Molière died, he persuaded the king to turn over to him, for his own use, the theater Molière had used. The theater is in the midst of a beautiful garden, in the heart of Paris. Like the garden, the theater is called the *Palais-Royal* —The Royal Palace. The theater still exists, but it is no longer used for ballet. Now, it is the home of the French National Theater, the *Comédie Française*, which combined Molière's own troupe of players with a second troupe. And, although Molière has been dead nearly three hundred years, his plays are still given at the *Palais-Royal*.

BALLET IN A THEATER ! To some, the idea seemed brilliant. But others thought it foolish.

At court ballets, they pointed out, the spectators lined three sides of the hall, forming a kind of horseshoe. In a theater, all spectators are in front of the dancers.

And then there was the proscenium arch, which framed the stage. Wouldn't that limit the view, too? Who could see around it?

The dancers quickly and easily solved such problems. They simply faced straight ahead.

To face front in this way was perfectly natural when the dancers moved forward—or backward—on the stage. But to move sideways over the stage, while still facing forward, meant that the dancer must cross one foot in front of the other. If his feet pointed ahead as he crossed them, he would be as awkward as a stumbling peasant. If he turned them out, though—as he had learned to do—his feet would never get tangled up.

In the same way, if the dancer pointed his feet before him as he posed in an *attitude* or an *arabesque*, his body

Seconde Journée

Theatre fait dans la mesme allée, sur lequel la Comedie, et le Ballet
de la Princesse d'Elide furent representés.

1680. Ballet in a theater, where the proscenium arch limited the view? The dancer's turned out position made it possible.

would seem bent out of shape. But if he turned his feet, knees, and hips outward, his body had the beauty of a Greek statue.

That turned-out position had been used in dance for nearly three hundred years. But it had been used for completely different reasons. Still, it was the basis of all dances at both balls and courts. Without that turnout, ballet could never have been performed in a theater. And once it came to theaters, far more people could enjoy it than ever had before.

When ballets were danced at the courts, only people who were invited were permitted to watch it. Even when a marvelous theater was built at Versailles by Louis XV, the son of Louis the Great, no tickets were sold. No one entered that theater unless asked by the king. And no one—ever—applauded unless the king applauded first.

When ballet and operas and plays were performed in the theaters of Paris, or in other cities, it was different. Then anyone who could afford a ticket was welcome. They were often the same aristocrats who were invited to the court ballets. Now, though, people of the middle class also went to the theater. They were bankers and traders and merchants. They were not of noble birth. Many, though, were very wealthy. Bringing ballet into the theater was one more great step forward in its development. This time, though, it was due to Lully and not the king.

But Lully soon had an even bolder notion. It was a notion that would change the entire future of ballet. The king's music master asked women to dance in the theaters. They would take the parts still played by young boys in all public performances. Women would take the parts of women!

As time went on, the rules for dance were set down in diagrams
and pictures. The dances were often complex, but they still
relied on the turned-out position.

The women who danced in public were all professionals. They danced because they were paid to. And they were considered to be without any shame at all. No lady—no woman of noble birth or any breeding at all—dreamed of appearing before people who bought tickets.

At the courts, though, the noblewomen still danced in those ballets performed for members of the court and their closest friends. And how it delighted them! For hundreds of years, gentlemen used the dance to show off a handsome leg, a slender figure. Now it was the ladies' turn to show off their tiny waists, their lovely shoulders. They, too, made dance an excuse to pose and preen before their admirers. They, too, used ballet to display their beauty. And they used it, too, as they always had, to display their wealth. For a ball, a noblewoman wore her most precious jewels, her costliest gown.

Even the gowns worn on ordinary occasions at court were heavy and difficult to manage. Those worn for the dance were far more so. They were made of the finest fabrics to be found. Even a young boy playing the part of a simple shepherd wore a costume of real satin. The gowns of the noblewomen might be fashioned of satin, too. Or they might be made of materials still more precious and not nearly so light.

They might be of heavy silk, or of rich brocades. They might be of luxurious velvet, soft and smooth but still a burden to carry. Often, too, the fabrics were shot through with threads of silver—real silver. Or with threads of gold—real gold. Just as often, they glistened with brilliants and beads, which were sewn to the bodices of their dresses or which bordered their full, wide skirts.

When she danced, every gentlewoman was laden with

The Genteel Manner of Position.

When noble ladies danced in their wide skirts, they held their hands in a delicate, graceful way.

exquisite jewels. Like the gold or the silver in the cloth of her gown, they were all real. And if the jewels were pinned at her waist, or on her skirt, her dress was heavier still. There was only one way that a lady could lift such a stiff and heavy skirt when she danced. That was by holding her arms in a curved position.

Ballet dancers still do that. Their costumes now are often as light as feathers. They are also very short. Yet dancers still curve their arms the way the ladies of the courts did, in order to hold up their skirts, more than two hundred years ago.

When they picked up their skirts, the noblewomen caught them between their thumbs and their middle fingers. The fingers formed a small, graceful circle.

They held their other fingers above—slightly curved—and out. And so the hand itself was graceful and elegant. This position of the hand called attention to its delicacy and beauty.

But it did more. Heavy though the fabrics of their gowns were, they were also fragile. Velvet crushed easily. Silk and satin were quickly smudged. So the position of the hand and the fingers, which was so flattering to the dancer, also protected her dress.

Today, most ballerinas—most of the time—wear very light clothing. Only once in a while does a dancer now catch up her skirt like a lady at court. But whether she does or not, and no matter what she wears, she still holds her hand just the way they did. Her thumb and middle finger meet to form a tiny circle. Her other fingers are lifted and slightly curved. They are elegant, and graceful.

A ballerina today holds her shoulders almost motionless. Once more she is imitating the ladies of the court. If those ladies rarely moved their shoulders, it was again because of their gowns. The skirts to those gowns were wide and full. They came to just above the instep and revealed very little. But the tops of the gowns, the bodices, revealed a great deal, just as they were meant to.

Necklines were cut very low and very wide. They displayed the long, slender necks of the gentlewomen. They also showed off their lovely white shoulders. Sleeves were set into the bodices to bare as much of the shoulder as possible. They were long and tight and adorned with rows and rows of lace. Ribbons threaded through the lace made the sleeves still tighter. And both drew attention to the loveliness of a lady's arms.

Such tight sleeves and an even tighter bodice held the

shoulders steady, fixed. If the ladies did not move them, very often it was because they could not. But that hardly mattered. The low-cut gown and the tight sleeves, the tiny waist set off by a full skirt, the form-fitting bodice all did what they were intended to do. They showed the elegance of the wearer. They showed her grace. They showed her beauty.

PIERRE BEAUCHAMPS, the dancing master of King Louis XIV, gave ballet its rules. Then the ladies of the courts gave ballet some more of its traditions. And both would be followed in many countries.

Before long, every king, every prince—even dukes and barons—set up his own ballet company. Those in very small states, which were not yet nations, were very small. But they were very important. Others were founded by the rulers of the most powerful countries in Europe.

One of the first to appear was in England. The Royal Danish Ballet, in the fairy-tale city of Copenhagen, followed soon after. Italy had two ballet companies, and two opera companies. One, in the south, was in Naples. The other, in the north, was in Milan.

Then came Vienna, in Austria. And Stuttgart, a small court in Germany. And Sweden. And finally the great Imperial Russian Ballet. The czar, Peter the Great, loved dance so much that he built a theater for a ballet company in Moscow. Then he built a second theater for a second company in St. Petersburg, the capital.

Ballet was performed everywhere, always the way it was in France at the time of Louis XIV. The rules and the traditions of those days were followed faithfully, but over the years it developed so that it seemed quite different from what it once was.

Before Louis XIV, the development was due to the dancing masters. After him it was due to the dancers. Most of them were women, the ballerinas.

Not every woman who danced—not even every woman who danced leading roles—was a "ballerina." Only the very best among them were given that name.

To become a very good dancer took, and still takes, many hours of practice every day. To become a ballerina took many more hours. Moreover, the dancer needed a very special talent to succeed, and she had to begin her training when she was still very young. From the time she was a child, the ballerina devoted much of her life to ballet. One, Marie Sallé, was still only a child when she began performing in public. Although Sallé was French, she first danced in London. The year was 1716. Sallé was just nine years old.

That was astonishing enough. What was more astonishing was the way she was dressed. Sallé did not wear the usual heavy, tight-waisted ballgown. She did not wear a full skirt—stuffed and puffed at the hips with wire and whalebone—like other dancers. She did not wear an enormous, top-heavy wig. Instead, her hair hung down straight, in the most natural way. She did not even wear jewels.

Marie Sallé's costume, instead, was as plain as possible. It was made of muslin and was modeled on the tunic worn by men and women in ancient Greece. It fell from her shoulders and was draped softly around her body. And it

1707–1856. Marie Sallé, the first great ballerina.

was short. It was short enough to give the audience a glimpse of Sallé's legs.

They were shocked. But they were impressed, too, because Marie Sallé, in her soft and flowing gown, danced with an ease and a naturalness they had never seen before. It was not long before she was a favorite of both the English public and the French.

Marie Sallé continued to dance for many years. Although she no longer gave the audience a glimpse of her legs, she did wear light, loose clothing. And because she did, she was able to skim along the surface of the stage. Her leaps, her jumps, were nothing compared to those of today's dancers. Yet, compared to others of her time, they were marvels of lightness. When Marie Sallé danced, she seemed to float on the air.

An even greater favorite of the French public was a dancer from Spain. Her full name was so long—Marie Anne de Cupis de Camargo—that no one used it. Instead she was known only as Camargo.

Like Marie Sallé, Camargo created a sensation and for much the same reason. Sallé, as a child, had shown her legs. Camargo, as a woman and a full-fledged ballerina, shortened her skirts.

She did not shorten them much; she raised them only a few inches above the floor. But her ankles could be seen and, what was more important, her feet.

And it was important that Camargo's feet be seen. She had gone beyond even Sallé in performing new and difficult steps.

Camargo beat her feet together in midair. She crossed and uncrossed them and crossed them again in a step called an *entrechat*. (That word, too, is French. Its literal meaning is "to chase between.") She whipped from one foot to the other, moving forward or backward or to the side. She was as light and as fleet as a small bird.

Then Camargo found a way to make every step lighter still. She found a way to move with such ease, such grace that it seemed she almost soared.

Centuries earlier, ladies and gentlemen began to wear leather shoes with leather soles to protect their feet from

1710–1770. "Camargo" . . . the first ballerina to dance "in the air," the style of ballet today.

cobblestones. Then they began to wear clogs, to protect their shoes. Then, to be more elegant, they made the clogs smaller and smaller until they were only heels. Ever since then, ladies and gentlemen had worn shoes or slippers with heels on them. Now Camargo took her heels off. When she did, she seemed to soar. And so every ballet dancer since has worn soft slippers, slippers without heels.

When knights and nobles first danced in the halls of the castles, dance was divided into two types. In one type —in the more solemn and stately dances—their feet merely glided across the polished floors. They did not leave the floor. This was the *basse*—or low—dance. In ballet, this type of dance was called *danse terre à terre*—dance close to the ground.

Sometimes, though, the courtiers took tiny leaps, made little jumps, skipped or hopped. When they did—when their feet left the floor—the dance was called *haute*—high.

But when Camargo took the heels off her slippers, she danced so far above the floor that the word "high" had no meaning. And so her style of dance was called *dans l'air*—in the air. It is the style of ballet today.

Today, dancers sometimes seem to rise far above the stage. They seem to have wings. They seem to fly. Like Camargo, they dance *dans l'air*.

Not quite like Camargo, though. Today, dancers go far beyond Camargo. And far higher, as well.

THERE WERE OTHER GREAT BALLERINAS,
after Marie Sallé and Camargo. Each brought a new and
special touch to ballet. They jumped higher; they spun
around more quickly. And audiences loved them.

While ballerinas were bringing new ideas about dance
to the way they performed it, others were bringing new
ideas to the stories ballet told. And these new ideas were
only keeping pace with the new ideas in the world itself.

At the time of Catherine de Medici, just as at the time
of Lorenzo, the stories of ballet were taken from ancient
myths. The same was true of the stories of ballets performed during the time of Henry IV and of Louis XIII
and of Louis XIV. They all told of gods and goddesses
who took the form of human beings. They told of nymphs
and naiads. They told of imaginary creatures.

But after the time of Louis XIV, people lost interest in
the ancient world and in its myths. Now their attention
was caught by a very real world. It was a world, though,
that was very far away.

People had dreamed of distant places for centuries.
Many went beyond the dream and sailed across the sea to

discover for themselves what lay beyond. Two hundred years before the English defeated the French at Agincourt, Marco Polo, an Italian, explored China. He came back with the most amazing tales of that strange and mysterious land.

Other explorers followed the daring Marco Polo. They too returned to tell of amazing adventures. And before long, poets wrote about those faraway places. Artists painted them. And ballet masters created ballets about the fascinating lands halfway around the world.

India! Turkey! China! Peru! How exciting they were to people of the eighteenth and nineteenth centuries. Almost none would see them for themselves. Very few would even know what they were really like. But that hardly mattered. They could imagine them and so they did. And they put them, just as they imagined them, into the theater.

Turks with brightly colored turbans on their heads took the places of Greek gods in helmets. Savages with painted faces took the places of nymphs and naiads. Satyrs and Tritons and Sirens disappeared. Now there were Arabs in fezzes and baggy trousers.

But there were other changes, more important changes, taking place in the world. And before long they swept away the Turks and the Arabs and the savages.

These changes were brought about in protest to the great luxury at the courts and especially at the courts of the French kings. These monarchs had built huge palaces. They entertained lavishly, and their guests were numbered in the thousands. They spent fortunes on jewels, for themselves and for their friends. And they fought one costly war after another.

1727–1810. Jean Georges Noverre completely reformed ballet by stripping dance of everything false and stiff.

The money for their palaces came from taxes. The money for their entertainments came from taxes. The money for their wars came from taxes. And the more they spent, the higher those taxes rose.

As their taxes went up, the people of France began to grumble. As taxes continued to mount, the grumbling grew louder. And when they were so high that people could no longer pay—when they, themselves, went hungry—they revolted against the king. They overthrew him.

Louis XIV had been dead for many years. But the reigning King, Louis XVI, and his Queen, Marie Antoinette, were both put to death. Thousands of other nobles were put to death, too. A new government was set up. It was dedicated to the ideals of *Liberté, Egality, Fraternité*. Liberty, Equality, Brotherhood.

There were other revolutions in other lands. Other kings were overthrown. A new spirit blew through Europe like a strong wind. It blew away many of the old ideas.

People were tired of the fine manners and the fine clothes of the courts. They were tired of elegance. They were pleased only by whatever was simple and natural.

Philosophers were proclaiming an "age of reason." And to them the extremes of the court were far from reasonable.

They praised the average, the common man. He might be a peasant, unable to read or write or even speak correctly. He might have no manners at all. He might seem little more than a savage.

But that was exactly what made him worthy. He was a "noble savage" because he was true to his own nature. He did not pretend to be what he was not, like members of the aristocracy.

Even before the French Revolution, one ballet master held the same views. His name was Jean Georges Noverre, and it is as important in ballet as that of Pierre Beauchamps.

Noverre tried to simplify ballet. He tried to do away with everything that was affected or unnecessary.

Men still wore masks on stage. Noverre had them take them off. He spoke out against the coils of wire and the strips of whalebone that held out women's wide skirts. He asked them to wear lighter clothes instead, almost like that which both Sallé and Camargo would wear later.

And Noverre turned back to the ideas of Balthasar.

Too often the purpose of ballet was forgotten. Too often it served only to show off certain dancers and not to tell a story.

The story may have been Noverre's greatest interest. It did not have to be true, but it had to be a story people would believe. It had to be clear and it had to be simple.

The same was true of the pantomime—the gestures—that helped to tell the story. They could not be stiff; they could not be false or so extreme that they were absurd.

Jean Georges Noverre did not succeed in what he hoped to do. He did not reform ballet during his days as a ballet master.

But the French Revolution succeeded where Noverre failed. It swept away all that was false and exaggerated. It made ballet simple and natural. And Noverre himself lived to see it.

In this ballet by Noverre, a dramatic moment is heightened by the greater honesty and simplicity he brought to ballet.

XIV

THE FRENCH REVOLUTION changed the way people there were governed. France became a republic, like America.

But the French republic lasted only a short time. The country had long been at war and those wars continued. And new ones broke out when other kings, who were afraid the Revolution would spread, attacked France.

The armies defending France were led by a young Corsican. His name was Napoleon Bonaparte and he started his military career as a lowly corporal. But he quickly rose to the rank of general.

Napoleon was ambitious and he was ruthless. Only ten years after Louis XVI was executed, he proclaimed himself ruler of France. Five years later, in 1804, he was crowned as emperor. The French Republic—the first of five—was dead.

Although France was once more ruled by a monarch, life under Napoleon was far different from life under the king. The royal palaces had been seized and stripped of their treasures. The great estates had been broken up. Most of the nobles had been executed like the king or had fled.

The people who counted in France now were not those of high rank. They were those who were wealthy. The size of a man's bank account was far more important than his birth or breeding.

The French Revolution sparked other revolutions. Because of them, the way people were governed changed in many countries of Europe.

At the same time another revolution, of another kind, was taking place. It changed the way people lived. This other revolution was accomplished without war and without bloodshed. It took place in most of the countries of western Europe. Its greatest effect was probably in England. This revolution was called the "Industrial Revolution."

The Industrial Revolution began when machines were invented to do work that had always been done by hand before. It began when factories were built in which to do the work that had always been done at home.

Machines were fast; a single one could turn out as much work in a day as a woman sewing or weaving at home could in months. Suddenly, those who worked in their own cottages knew they could no longer earn their livings there. And so they left for the cities and the factories.

But life in the cities was harsh and ugly for the poor. They worked long hours in dark and dreary places, then went home to rooms which were even darker, even drearier. Small children were forced to work in the factories, and sick people tended their machines until they died.

These people were free. Yet their lives were as miserable as those of serfs and peasants who toiled for the lords

1845. Romantic ballet reached its height when the four leading ballerinas of the day danced together in their Pas de Quatre.

of the manors hundreds of years before. In some ways, their lives were worse. When peasants were bound to the land, it was the duty of the lord to protect them. But no one protected the poor who worked in the factories.

Centuries before, when life was too frightening to

bear, knights invented the world of chivalry. In that world, women were pure and good. If the nobles devoted themselves to proving that they were worthy of such women, they could shut out the horrors around them. They forgot about death and disease and starvation by writing poems to their ladies.

Much the same happened during the Industrial Revolution. Because the real world was one of filth and poverty and cruelty, people looked for a different one. And artists gave it to them.

They let their imaginations run wild when they wrote their books and plays and poems, when they painted their pictures. They appealed to people's feelings, not to their minds. And they created a fantasy world in which everything was pure and good and close to perfect.

In that world, love was more important than duty or honor. The world the artists created was a romantic world.

So still another revolution took place in the early years of the nineteenth century. It was a revolution in the way people looked at the world. Because it ushered in the period of time called "The Romantic Era," it was called "The Romantic Revolution."

No form of art was better suited to the new ideas than ballet. People everywhere—in France and Germany and Denmark, too—filled theaters to watch it and to escape into a dream world for a few hours. And nowhere was ballet more popular than in England.

These romantic ballets told tales of love. Their stories were those of beautiful maidens whose hearts were captured by handsome princes. Sometimes they were peasant girls; sometimes fairy creatures or ghostly spirits. Often they were betrayed by their lovers. If they were, they simply vanished as mysteriously as they appeared. No one looked for reality in ballet. Instead they asked for something—anything—to make them forget it.

In the make-believe world of ballet, women were as perfect as they were in the days of chivalry. They belonged to the world of spirits, not to earth. They did not walk or run, but floated through the air, light as clouds. And no ballerina seemed so light, so cloudlike as Marie Taglioni, who was born in 1804, almost a hundred years after Sallé and Camargo.

Taglioni was considered the greatest dancer of her time. Many think she was the greatest ever. Her ideas shaped ballet more than those of any other ballerina. Her style was that of Camargo. Like Camargo, she danced *dans l'air*. But how she developed that style! How much she added that was her very own!

She copied Camargo when she wore slippers without heels. But Taglioni's shoes were far lighter than those of earlier ballerinas. And so she was able to dance on the tips of her toes—on *pointe*. She was among the first to dance in this way.

Taglioni's slippers were almost like gloves, fitting close to the foot. They had no stiffening, like shoes worn by dancers now. Instead, they were made only of light strips of silk ribbon woven together. Whatever support her slippers gave her came from the patches of darning on the tips of them and from the ribbons that were tied around the ankle. Taglioni could balance on her toes in these slippers. She could even take a few quick steps. But she could not stay on her toes very long, or perform any of the many complicated steps that are so common today.

1804–1884. Marie Taglioni, the first ballerina to dance on pointe—*on toe.*

Like Marie Sallé and like Camargo, Taglioni danced in a costume that surprised her audience. Hers was far different from either of theirs, though. It was designed especially for her and was just a tight-fitting bodice with a skirt of light gauze attached.

That costume became the classic costume of ballet. It is called a *tutu*, and is familiar to every audience today. Now it is often quite short. Sometimes it is only a stiff tulle ruffle around the dancer's hips. But Taglioni's *tutu*—and those of dancers of her time—fell to just below her knees. Because it was so much lighter than the usual gown—even those of Sallé and Camargo—it gave the ballerina far more freedom as she moved. When she danced on her toes in her filmy white skirts, she truly seemed to fly *"dans l'air."*

One new ballet after another was created during this time. All were in the romantic spirit. There was a simplicity to the dancing. And the settings were those of nature herself. Shady glens and leafy dells were the backdrops for the dances of wraiths and sprites and spirits.

The settings for romantic ballets may have been taken from nature. But, as in the court ballets, scenery and stage devices were used for the most spectacular effects. Clouds floated above the dells; grottos were hidden within them. Flowers blossomed before the eyes of the audience; evil witches disappeared in flames.

It was 1681 when Jean-Baptiste Lully persuaded women to appear in public in a ballet, *The Triumph of Love*. A hundred and fifty years later, they starred in ballets created especially for them. Scores of lovely young girls danced with the ballerinas. They made up the *corps de ballet*. And, like an army marching in step, the entire group moved as one.

Such *corps* are not new to dance. They went back, too, to the court ballets of Catherine de Medici. One of the first—a group of sixteen young girls—had astonished the Polish Ambassadors. Another group danced the first *entrée* at the ballet for Queen Louise.

Though the male dancers of the Romantic Era were unimportant, Petipa went on to become a great choreographer in Russia. Here, at an earlier date, he partnered the famous ballerina, Carlotta Grisi.

The dancers of the *corps de ballet*, like the ballerina, were all dressed in *tutus*. That costume gave a special name to these ballets. They were called *ballet-blanc*— "white ballet."

Even those who danced the roles of mortals wore *tutus*. Only the apron stitched to this dancer's skirt showed that she was a peasant. Only the tiny crown on the head of another showed that she was a princess.

Princesses and peasant girls—ballerinas—held the spotlight in the romantic ballet. While there were many fine male dancers, they never gained the fame of the women. They never became the idols of the public, like the ballerinas.

Today, the court ballets have been forgotten. The men who partnered the romantic ballerinas in the early 1800s are not remembered for their dancing either, though many are remembered as teachers and as choreographers.

But the ballerinas are remembered. And the ballets they danced are remembered, too. And many—*La Sylphide* and *Giselle* and *Coppélia* are still performed. They are so beautiful, and the ballerinas who danced them were so lovely, that another name was given to those early years of the nineteenth century. It was called "the golden age of ballet."

A GOLDEN AGE CANNOT LAST FOREVER. The golden age of ballet did not. In a little more than fifty years it was over. But what a marvelous age it was!

Inspired choreographers created great ballets. They were danced by the most talented and the best-trained ballerinas. And both the choreographers and the dancers brought brilliant new ideas to their work.

They wove a magic spell together. Through dance, they blotted out the dreary everyday world. They brought happiness to everyone who could pay a few pennies for a seat in the balcony.

There were many people too poor to pay even a few pennies—or a few *sous*—for such enchantment. But there were still very many who could afford that much for such delight. And they crowded into the theaters.

Ballets were given everywhere in Europe. Opera had become the favorite entertainment in France and Italy and Germany; ballet, though, was close behind it.

Because ballet was so popular, every opera had to include one at some point. They were short ballets. And they had nothing to do with the story. They were really *inter-*

mezzi—or *intermédes*—or *entremets*. But as in the days of Lully, any opera without one was bound to fail.

The famous dancers, the greatest dancers, at last grew old; they could no longer perform the marvelous *jétés* and *pirouettes*—the leaps and turns— that made audiences gasp. New dancers tried to take their places. But none had the genius of the older ones. And so they merely copied Taglioni and Camargo and Sallé—and Fanny Elssler and Carlotta Grisi and Fanny Cerrito. Their dancing had none of the deep feeling of the great ballerinas. It was just a series of tricks.

The men who had planned the great ballets, the choreographers, grew old, too. Those who followed them lacked inspiration. And they, too, merely copied the masters. Even the music for the new ballets was dull. Too many composers ground out too many scores in too short a time. And the music for one ballet sounded like that for a dozen others.

Ballet, once so alive, became a bore. People grew tired of seeing the same thing over and over. So they turned to more exciting amusements. The golden age of ballet was over, at least in Western Europe. But in Russia it was as glorious as ever.

In almost every way, Russia was a backward country. People still lived as serfs, as they had five hundred years before in France. They were still bound to the land. They still owed allegiance to the noble, the lord of the estate they lived on.

Russia had not been touched by the Industrial Revolution. Machines were unknown. And Russia was still ruled by a monarch, the Czar. He was a tyrant who held absolute power.

The Czar and his nobles lived in great splendor. But the country had never developed the arts—music, painting or literature. They looked to the West, and especially to France, for that.

The wealthy Russians—and only the nobles were wealthy—brought men and women from France to teach their children. They brought chefs to cook their banquets. They brought the china and the crystal used at those banquets from France. They even spoke French instead of their own language.

And they brought ballet from France, too.

The Revolution swept away the courts of France. But those of Russia survived. They were more splendid and more luxurious than ever. Life went on in the nineteenth century just as it did at the time of Peter the Great.

Ballet was very much a part of that life. It was not presented at the courts in Russia; it never had been. Instead it was performed in the theaters, as it was in the West. But in Russia it was still fresh, still original. Now it was the turn of the Russians to create marvelous new ballets. They were all in the romantic style. And they, too, are still performed.

The ballet masters who thought of these great Russian ballets came from France. But Russian musicians were at last being trained in the schools of St. Petersburg and Moscow. One, Peter Ilich Tschaikowsky, wrote the music for *Swan Lake* and *The Nutcracker*. No ballets are better loved. And few are performed more often.

But in Russia, too, ballet became dull and stale. Dancers turned into acrobats. Ballets repeated the same steps, the same scenes, and always in the same pattern.

All that was changed by a group of young dancers with ideas which, to the Russian authorities, smacked of

1891–1931. Anna Pavlova, the Russian ballerina who has become a legend.

rebellion. Yet they were really the ideas of Noverre and of Balthasar, too.

The first to state them was a twenty-year-old, Michel Fokine. For him, the story was the very reason for ballet. Everything in it must be used to tell that story; the steps themselves, the order of the dances, even the costumes and music and scenery.

As for movement, it must suit the subject of the ballet. It must suit the time and the place of the ballet, too. And it must be much freer. Even the head and the arms should move more freely. Pantomime should be simple. It should be easily understood. And the whole body should be used, not the hands alone. Ballet was not meant to display the beauty or the ability of a dancer. It was music. It was drama. It was art.

The Russian authorities listened, in their way, to Fokine. They even let him present his own dances. But he showed them only at student recitals. Then, to rid themselves of this nuisance, those same authorities let him go to Paris for a summer season. With him were some of the finest dancers from the Imperial School of Ballet. Among those dancers were two who became legends. One was the ballerina, Anna Pavlova. The other was Vaslav Nijinsky. He may have been the greatest male dancer of all time.

All were invited to Paris by a Russian nobleman, Serge Diaghileff. He had been a lawyer and had studied music, too. Now he was an impresario; he arranged concerts and put on plays—and ballets.

Diaghileff shared Fokine's views. Moreover, he believed that only the most talented people could create such ballets. And so he hired them. The artists who painted the scenery—even the curtain—and designed the costumes were the leading artists in Paris. Many were Russian. The composers were the leading composers. And the greatest of them, Igor Stravinsky, was Russian, too.

But Diaghileff did not depend on composers of the day. Some ballets were set to music by earlier composers. And many of Fokine's most exciting ballets were danced to the music of those Russian composers who used folk tunes and rhythms in their scores.

From the very first performance, the "Russian Ballets" were a triumph. Audiences were thrilled by the bril-

1890–1950. The Russian, Vaslaf Nijinsky, may have been the greatest of all male dancers.

liant colors of the scenery, so different from the dull greens and browns they were used to. They were thrilled by the costumes. The white *tutu* was gone. In its place, dancers wore robes and trousers and embroidered skirts fit for the Czar himself—or for the characters of the story.

They were thrilled by the movements of the dance; by the freedom of the gestures. And they were thrilled by the dancers themselves. Each was a master of the technique of classical ballet. And each was using that technique in a new, flowing and expressive style.

That night was more than a triumph for Fokine and Diaghileff. It marked the beginning of a new era—the modern era—of ballet.

The Russian Ballets were seen season after season in Paris and in the West until World War I broke out. Before the war was over, a revolution took place in Russia. The Czar was overthrown, just as Louis XVI had been in France long before. And just as the nobles fled France at that time, the "White Russians," members of the nobility and their supporters, fled the country.

There were two very great dancers and choreographers among them. One was Leonide Massine. The second was George Balanchine. Like Fokine, they too went to Paris. And they too joined forces with Diaghileff, there in France.

How right it was that Russians should go to France to bring new life to ballet. It was there that ballet began when two other foreigners, a queen from Italy and her Italian ballet master, created the very first real one. It was there that a second Italian, a composer, moved ballet from the courts, where only a few saw it, to the theaters where so many would enjoy it. And now, when ballet had become so dull that it was dying out, another group of foreigners traveled all the way from Russia. They brought with them their talent, their ideas, their genius. And with those ideas, that talent, that genius, they restored the glory of dance.

Ballet today is far different from what it was at the time of Catherine de Medici. And dance is different from that of the balls in the castles in the years after Agincourt.

But there are many things that are still the same.

Those who look closely at a dancer poised to leap— his weight centered, his knees bent in a plié—will see behind him a noble ready for a duel.

Those who look closely as a ballerina moves slowly and elegantly across a stage, her feet turned out, her toes touching the floor first—will see behind her all the kings of France.